D0443730

WITHDRAWN

# THE ROAD TO FREEDOM

ALSO BY ARTHUR C. BROOKS

*The Battle*
*Who Really Cares*
*Gross National Happiness*

# THE ROAD TO
# FREEDOM

## HOW TO WIN THE FIGHT FOR FREE ENTERPRISE

### ARTHUR C. BROOKS

BASIC
BOOKS
A MEMBER OF THE PERSEUS BOOKS GROUP
NEW YORK

Copyright © 2012 by The American Enterprise Institute
Published by Basic Books,
A Member of the Perseus Books Group

Books published by Basic Books are available at special discounts for
bulk purchases in the United States by corporations, institutions, and
other organizations. For more information, please contact the Special
Markets Department at the Perseus Books Group, 2300 Chestnut Street,
Suite 200, Philadelphia, PA 19103, or call (800) 810-4145, ext. 5000, or
e-mail special.markets@perseusbooks.com.

Design and production by Eclipse Publishing Services
Set in 10-point Concorde

A CIP catalog record for this book is available
from the Library of Congress.

ISBN: 978-0-465-02940-2 (hc)
ISBN: 978-0-465-02941-9 (e-book)

10 9 8 7 6 5 4 3 2

*To the entrepreneurs around the world
who earn their success and create the opportunities
for the rest of us to earn ours.*

# CONTENTS

# I

# Making the Moral Case for Free Enterprise

# 1

## WHY MAKE THE MORAL CASE FOR FREE ENTERPRISE?

$A$re you satisfied or dissatisfied with the way the nation is being governed?

If you are like 81 percent of Americans, your answer is "dissatisfied."[1] Since that question was first asked in the early 1970s, dissatisfaction has never been higher. At the height of the Watergate scandal in 1974, it was only 66 percent. When the stock market crashed in 2008, it was 72 percent.

Some of the dissatisfied Americans are easy to spot. They gather on the Mall in Washington, D.C., for a Tea Party rally against the growth of government. Or they take over Zuccotti Park in lower Manhattan as part of an "Occupy Wall Street" demonstration against big government's codependent wife, corporate cronyism.

But these demonstrators are only a tiny portion of the quarter-billion dissatisfied Americans. The majority are ordinary people, too busy to attend a demonstration (let alone sleep in a park), but nonetheless simmering with frustration over what is happening to our country.

For years now, it seems as if America has been in decline, unable to pull out of an economic funk. The government has responded by bailing out powerful corporations that are "too big to fail" and delivering a stimulus package that doesn't seem to stimulate anything other than the government itself. Older Americans see the country they have loved their whole lives changing for the worse, and young people see their future prosperity vanishing into thin air.

So what's the solution? Some will tell you it's the 2012 election. In 2008, Americans elected a slate of politicians who promised solutions to growing national problems. But according to many economists and most measures of public opinion, the current administration has made those problems worse.[2] The 2012 election should be a chance to set things right. Right?

The 2012 election is important, to be sure. The continuation of many policies—from ObamaCare, to "Too Big to Fail," to Keynesian-style stimulus packages—is at stake.

But the election is not a panacea for all of the problems facing the country; it's not even close. If America's current malaise were the product of just three years of bad ideas and poor leadership, we could solve it by brooming out a bunch of politicians. Unfortunately, the predicament is the product of nearly a century of accumulated policy, and the solution won't come with one election.

Consider the crushing public debt. As I write these words in the fall of 2011, the national debt comes to $48,000 for every man, woman, and child in America.[3] One-third of that amount has accumulated during the past three years, but the rest of the debt existed before the current recession and the current administration. It is a long-standing, unwelcome, and bipartisan gift to our children and grandchildren. Government spending at all levels (federal, state, and local) amounted to 15 percent of GDP in 1940. In 1980, it was 30 percent. By 1990, it was 32 percent. Today, it is 36 percent. For many years, policy makers have turned this fly-wheel, and today it packs terrifying force.

The Congressional Budget Office tells us that by 2038, government spending will be 50 percent of GDP. Think about this for a moment. Americans will work from January 1 until June 30 each year just to pay for the government—a government that a large majority believes has too much power, tries to do too much, and provides unsatisfactory services.[4]

It's going to take a lot more than one election to get us off what Nobel laureate Friedrich Hayek called the "road to serfdom." Americans today are experiencing a low-grade, virtual servitude to an ever-expanding, unaccountable government that, starved for tax revenues, has appropriated for itself funds that entrepreneurs could have used to grow the economy, has created a protected class of government workers and crony corporations that play by a different set of rules than the rest of America, and has consequently left the nation in hock for generations to come.

Some believe this road inevitably leads us to one of two places: social democracy or long-term austerity. In the former case, the U.S. finally hits a tipping point where few people actually pay for their share of the growing government. At this point, the majority of Americans become truly invested in a social welfare state, which stabilizes at some very high level of taxation and government social spending. Think Norway or Holland.

But social democracy is expensive. It requires that America emerge successfully from the current economic crisis. If it doesn't, we get something worse, in which the welfare state collapses under its own weight. That is, at some point, citizens of the world wise up and stop lending the U.S. money, or at least stop lending at relatively low interest rates. In the second scenario, your kids are poorer than you, and their kids poorer than them. Think Greece, Spain, Portugal, and Ireland. After years of deficit spending, these failing welfare states have become unsustainable, forcing their citizens to endure severe austerity. Spanish youth unemployment today is almost 50 percent, and about half of adults under age thirty-five live with their parents.[5] In Greece, the general unemployment rate is 17 percent and quickly rising, and the government's external debt is projected to hit 190 percent of GDP by 2014.[6] Yet, after years of this misery, the citizens of these countries know no other way but to clamor for even more government solutions that effectively steal their children's future.

In other words, either social democracy wins, or we all lose. We need to get off this road. But I believe it's going to take a cultural reformation to do so—a return to our founding ideals of free enterprise. This book is my attempt to show how.

WHAT IS FREE ENTERPRISE? It is the system of values and laws that respects private property and limits government, encourages competition and industry, celebrates achievement based on merit, and creates individual opportunity. Under free enterprise, people can pursue their own ends, and they reap the rewards and consequences, positive and negative, of their own actions.[7] Free enterprise requires trust in markets to produce the most desirable outcomes for society. It is the opposite of *statism*, which is the belief that the government is generally the best, fairest, and most trustworthy entity to distribute resources and coordinate our economic lives.

At first glance, moving America back toward free enterprise should be simple. Two years ago, I published a book showing that about 70 percent of Americans say they love free enterprise. They favor it over all other alternatives and are proud of the fact that the nation is based on this ideal. Large majorities say they want less government than we currently have.[8]

But if that's true, why is the government today so bloated, so powerful, and so imperious? Why do Americans acquiesce to almost every expansion of government—beyond the boundaries of what the Founders intended, and beyond what they say they actually want? For example, the Obama administration's health-care reforms are unpopular with a majority of citizens, yet in a poll fielded by CBS News/*New York Times* in 2010, 64 percent of people said they thought that government should provide health insurance for everyone.[9]

This is a paradox, but not a mystery. On the one hand, citizens say they love free enterprise. On the other hand, they sure wouldn't mind a new government-funded rec center and maybe a few free prescription drugs, and politicians gladly oblige to win votes. Most people hardly have the time to consider the inconsistency between these things.

In America, the road to serfdom doesn't come from a knock in the night and a jackbooted thug. It comes from making one little compromise to the free enterprise system after another. Each sounds sort of appealing. No single one is enough to bring down the system. But add them all up, and here we are: 81 percent dissatisfied.

So what's the solution? How do we help Americans understand that unless they actively choose free enterprise and eschew big government, they will ultimately only get the latter? Some say Americans need to hear a more forceful argument than ever before about the economic superiority of free enterprise over the alternatives. In other words, capitalism's advocates need to yell louder that free enterprise makes us richer than statism. Master the numbers, make some charts, and show Americans the evidence.

As a think tank president, I wish that strategy were correct. Nothing would make my job easier. But that strategy isn't correct. Materialistic arguments for free enterprise have been tried again and again. They have failed to stem the tide of big government.

There's only one kind of argument that will shake people awake: a *moral* one. Free enterprise advocates need to build the *moral case* to remind Americans why the future of the nation is worth more to each of us than a few short-term government benefits. To get off the path to social democracy or long-term austerity, all of us who love freedom must be able to express what is written on our hearts about what our Founders struggled to give us, what the culture of free enterprise has brought to our lives, and about the opportunity society we want to leave our children.

A LOT OF PEOPLE are reluctant to talk about morals or make a moral case for anything in politics and policy. We're willing to talk about principles, perhaps. Values, maybe. But morals? Especially among conservatives, morality evokes unpleasant memories of the "culture wars" of the 1990s, which focused on schismatic issues like abortion and homosexuality. As a result, many who believe in free enterprise steer clear of all public moral arguments.

This is a mistake and a missed opportunity. A great deal of research shows that people from all walks of life demand a system that is morally legitimate, not just efficient.[10] The moral legitimacy of free enterprise depends largely on how the system enables people to flourish, whether the system is fair, and how the system treats the least fortunate in society.

Privately, free enterprise's champions talk about these things incessantly. While they generally believe in the need for a safety net, they celebrate capitalism because they believe that succeeding on merit, doing something meaningful, seeing the poor rise by their hard work and virtue, and having control over life are essential to happiness and fulfillment. But in public debate, they often fall back on capitalism's superiority to other systems just in terms of productivity and economic efficiency. What moves them is the story of their immigrant grandparents who came to America to be free; but what they talk about is the most efficacious way to achieve a balanced budget.

The dogged reliance on materialistic arguments is a gift to statists. It allows them to paint free enterprise advocates as selfish and motivated only by money. Those who would expand the government have successfully appropriated the language of morality for their own political ends; redistributionist policies, they have claimed to great effect, are fairer, kinder, and more virtuous.[11] Too frequently, the rejoinder to these moral claims has been either dumbfounded silence or even *more* data on economic growth and fiscal consolidation.

Average Americans are thus too often left with two lousy choices in the current policy debates: the moral left versus the materialistic right. The public hears a heartfelt redistributionist argument from the left that leads to the type of failed public policies all around us today. But sometimes it feels as if the alternative comes from morally bereft conservatives who were raised by wolves and don't understand basic moral principles.

No wonder the general public is paralyzed into inaction, even when dissatisfaction with government is at an all-time high. There just doesn't seem to be a good alternative to the "statist quo," and as a consequence, the country is slipping toward a system that few people actually like. Most people, for instance, intuitively understand the urgent need for entitlement reform. But do you seriously expect Grandma to sit idly by and let free-marketeers tinker with her Medicare coverage so her great grandkids can get a slightly better mortgage rate? Not a chance—at least, not without a moral reason.

AMERICANS HAVE actually forgotten what the Founders knew well. They understood the need to make the moral argument for freedom, and they were not afraid to do so. In fact, they put a moral promise front and center in the Declaration of Independence:

> We hold these truths to be self-evident, that all men
> are created equal, that they are endowed by their
> Creator with certain unalienable Rights, that among
> these are Life, Liberty and the pursuit of Happiness.[12]

These famous words were not entirely original. Less than a month before Jefferson drafted the Declaration of Independence for the United States, George Mason wrote the Virginia Declaration of Rights, containing this passage:

> That all men are by nature equally free and inde-
> pendent, and have certain inherent rights, of which,
> when they enter into a state of society, they cannot,
> by any compact, deprive or divest their posterity;
> namely, the enjoyment of life and liberty, with the
> means of acquiring and possessing property, and
> pursuing and obtaining happiness and safety.[13]

The emphasis on property came from the philosopher John Locke, who believed that all men had the natural rights to acquire, protect, and dispose of property. But Jefferson decided to focus just on the *pursuit of happiness* instead.

The shift in emphasis away from material property and toward the pursuit of happiness was a shift from materialism to morality. America was intended as the greatest experiment in liberty in the history of the world. Property was the "what" of this experiment. The pursuit of happiness was the "why." When asked years later what explained this formulation, Jefferson called it "an expression of the American mind."[14] In truth, it was an expression of the American heart—and still is.

The Founders did not promise happiness itself, only its pursuit, leaving it to us to define happiness any way we see fit, matching our skills with our passions. This was the moral promise of the nation to its people: the promise of life and liberty that would allow the possibility of self-realization to a virtuous people.

We rarely contemplate how radical the promise of the pursuit of happiness is. And indeed, the closest our allies ever came to America's New Age creed was "liberté, égalité, fraternité" (liberty, equality, fraternity) in France; "life, liberty, and prosperity" in Australia; and from our Canadian cousins, "peace, order, and good government." (Inspiring, eh?)

This is not to say that Americans are the only people capable of making the moral case for freedom. At about the same time Jefferson was writing the Declaration, other pioneers in freedom were making the same argument in Europe. Adam Smith, the father of modern economics, did not just offer his audience invisible hands and cold capitalist calculations. Seventeen years before *The Wealth of Nations*, Smith wrote *The Theory of Moral Sentiments*, in which he brilliantly argued that humans are social animals, and that their moral ideas and actions are thus an inherent aspect of their nature. Smith believed that if people were left free to live their lives as they saw fit but were forbidden to use force or fraud, mankind would naturally form a rich and fulfilling community. Smith made the moral case for freedom long before he made the economic case for it.

Anyone who reads the words of the Founders—or Adam Smith—cannot miss their keen emphasis on the morality of the systems they intended to create. Our ideas about free enterprise and liberty were born from a sense of what is right and what helps us to thrive as people, not from a monomaniacal obsession with what makes us rich.

MORAL ARGUMENTS for freedom have always proven more powerful than material ones in moving ordinary people around the world to act in courageous ways. Evidence of this fact is everywhere. Consider the case of Tunisia's recent revolution.

In the last days of 2010, few people had ever heard of Mohamed Bouazizi. He was just a twenty-six-year-old street vendor in the Tunisian town of Sidi Bouzid who sold vegetables, as he had done since the age of ten. Each day, he would buy vegetables at the supermarket, load them into his wooden cart, and push the cart two kilometers to the city where he would sell them to passersby.[15]

The local people knew and liked Bouazizi because, despite his own poverty, he gave free vegetables to families who were even poorer than his own. The trouble he had was with the police, who made his life miserable. They constantly harassed and bullied him— regularly confiscating his produce and scales, humiliating him in public, and fining him for various arbitrary offenses against the bureaucratic codes that governed commercial life in Tunisia.

On December 17, 2010, a policewoman stopped Bouazizi on his way to the market—par for the course for the past sixteen years of his life. She demanded that he give her his scale. On this day, for some reason, Bouazizi decided he had had enough—and he refused. Shocked by his insubordination, the police officer slapped him and called in reinforcements who pushed him to the ground. In a show of raw power intended to crush his will, they took away not just his scale but all his merchandise as well.

Bouazizi walked to the city hall and asked to meet with an official for recourse. He was denied even a meeting. What came next shocked the world. Bouazizi went to a local store, bought a can of paint thinner, and returned to the street in front of city hall. He soaked himself in fuel and set himself on fire. He died eighteen days later.

The fire that burned Bouazizi to death ignited the Tunisian revolution. Tunisians rose up against the police, the kleptocratic bureaucrats, and the president who had given them license to crush honest men like Bouazizi. Within a month, they had scattered the police and arrested the president.

The story of Mohamed Bouazizi is not primarily economic; it is *moral*. Bouazizi didn't set himself on fire because he wanted to make more money. He did so to make a point about his right to live his life and take care of his family, free from arbitrary harassment. The Tunisian people rose up in moral revolt. The policewoman, the government officials of Tunisia, and their corrupt president were morally degenerate, and revolution was what they deserved. Although the initial dispute was over commerce, it was not money that inspired the uprising. Indeed, the rebels' slogan was "dignity before bread!"

Around the world, it is the moral case, not an economic one, that leads people to take risks for freedom. The collapse of the

Soviet Union was not due to the arms race or ruinous economic planning, as many in the West believe. It was the outcome of a moral belief that swept through the population and eventually penetrated the Soviet leadership itself. Premier Mikhail Gorbachev declared *glasnost* (openness) and democratization to be the foundation of his *perestroika* (restructuring) of Soviet society. "A new moral atmosphere is taking shape in the country," he declared. "A reappraisal of values and their creative rethinking is under way." For Gorbachev, this was not a pragmatic policy to maximize incomes and outputs; he called it his "moral position."[16]

In American politics and public policy, the same has always held true. Advances in the cause of freedom and free enterprise—while less dramatic than the collapse of communism—have succeeded when advocates have made a compelling moral case for it.

Consider the Reagan revolution of the 1980s. Ronald Reagan came into office with a landslide victory over Jimmy Carter in 1980, after Carter's deeply unpopular handling of virtually all areas of policy, from economics to national defense. Central to Reagan's victory was his celebration of free enterprise *as a moral system*—not simply a financial one. In his words, "The responsibility of freedom presses us towards higher knowledge and, I believe, moral and spiritual greatness. Through lower taxes and smaller government, government has its ways of freeing people's spirits. But only we, each of us, can let the spirit soar against our own individual standards. Excellence is what makes freedom ring."[17]

In the 1990s, welfare reform was likewise achieved through *moral* argument. The American welfare system had expanded enormously in the post–World War II period, largely directing financial and other support to fatherless families in poverty. Critics of the system argued that in addition to costing taxpayers hundreds of millions of dollars a year, generations of Americans were alienated from the workforce as a result.[18] Whole classes defined themselves as claimants on the U.S. government, and millions were consigned to squalid government housing and dignity-stripping income programs. Welfare programs created a permanent underclass: the unemployed received unearned support, lost job skills (or never acquired them), and thus became unable to gain stable employment, making them chronically, miserably, reliant on state aid.

Hundreds of years before, Thomas Jefferson cautioned that "dependence begets subservience and venality, suffocates the germ of virtue, and prepares fit tools for the designs of ambition."[19] Even Franklin Roosevelt had warned in his 1935 State of the Union address that "continued dependence on [government support] induces a spiritual and moral disintegration fundamentally destructive to the national fiber. To dole out relief in this way is to administer a narcotic, a subtle destroyer of the human spirit."[20]

With Jefferson's and Roosevelt's moral admonitions forgotten, the American welfare system grew and grew throughout the 1970s. Many leaders complained that it was a colossal waste of money, but their complaints were insufficient to make any meaningful change.

What finally changed the system was an influential book, entitled *Losing Ground*, by social scientist Charles Murray. Published in 1984, *Losing Ground* made the argument that the problem with the welfare system was not primarily an economic one. The problem was moral. The welfare policies of the 1960s changed the rules of the game for poor people, making it rational in the short term to behave in ways that would ensure poverty and dependency in the long term. "The most troubling aspect of social policy toward the poor," Murray wrote, "is not how much it costs, but what it has bought."[21]

Welfare had two pernicious effects, according to Murray. First, the system effectively held people in miserable conditions, harming those it was supposed to help. This was immoral and had to stop. Second, by holding people in this condition, the system created dependency on the state, stripping people of the dignity that comes from earning their own way. Once again, this was immoral because it hurt the recipients themselves.

Such arguments were radical in the mid-1980s. It took more than ten years—as major policy reforms always tend to take—but the moral case for welfare reform ultimately won the day and was even embraced by a Democratic president. During the Clinton administration, legislation was crafted to reduce the extent to which people could become dependent on the system. It did so by imposing time limits on how long people could receive support and requiring them to work to receive benefits. Welfare reform was signed into law in 1996.[22]

Welfare reform was a resounding success. According to the U.S. government, it helped to move 4.7 million Americans from welfare dependency to self-sufficiency within three years of enactment, and the welfare caseload declined by 54 percent between 1996 and 2004.[23] Even more importantly, there is evidence that it improved the lives of those who moved off welfare as a result. A new economic study using the General Social Survey shows that single mothers—despite lost leisure time and increased stress from finding child care and performing household duties while working—were significantly happier about their lives after reforms led them into the workforce.[24]

The point to remember here is this: Welfare reform was not passed when welfare became too expensive, but only when the moral case had been made that welfare was destroying the lives of the most vulnerable among us.

• • •

THIS BOOK IS my attempt to make the moral case for free enterprise and then apply that case to the leading policy issues of our day. If you have always believed free enterprise is the best system for America and are looking for the right arguments to win the debate, you will find those arguments in this book. And if you're not so sure free enterprise is the best answer for America, then I hope I might persuade you—as I have been persuaded.

I did not grow up committed to the free enterprise system— rather the opposite, in fact. I was raised in Seattle, one of the most progressive cities in America, in a family of artists and academics. No one in my world voted for Ronald Reagan. I had no friends or family who worked in business. I believed what most everybody in my world assumed to be true: that capitalism was a bit of a sham to benefit rich people, and the best way to get a better, fairer country was to raise taxes, increase government services, and redistribute more income.

I am a believer in free enterprise today only because of the studies I pursued starting in my twenties. I didn't go to a fancy university; I didn't even make it to college until I was twenty-eight years old and, then, only by correspondence courses at night. In a way, I got lucky; I didn't have to fit into any progressive campus social life, or impress any radical professors. I just had a stack of books on economics and a lot of data about the real world to study after I came home from work each day.

As I began to question my old views, some around me reacted with alarm. At one point when I was around age thirty, my mother took me aside and said, "Arthur, I need you to tell me the truth. . . . Have you been voting for Republicans?"

In truth, there had been no Road-to-Damascus political conversion experience, just a slow realization that what I thought I

18 THE ROAD TO FREEDOM

knew—about how to help the poor, about what made America different from other nations, and what gave people the best set of opportunities for their lives—didn't hold up to the evidence.

So I am not just a conservative ideologue or reflexive supporter of big business. In fact, I share the concerns of many on the left that freedom and opportunity are imperiled by corporate cronies, who inevitably are linked to the government through special deals and inside access. In this book, I'll argue that Washington's auto industry bailouts and its "Cash for Clunkers" program (handing out government grants to buy cars) are opposite sides of the same coin. Misbehavior on Wall Street was spawned by the predatory government-sponsored enterprises that started the housing crisis. Find me an opportunistic politician chumming the political waters with tax loopholes, and I'll show you a corporate shark.

I believe that if we want a better future, liberated from statism and corporate cronyism, the answer is the system that removes these shackles: free enterprise. In this book you will see why I have come to believe free enterprise is a beautiful, noble system—so revolutionary in an imperfect world—that rewards aspiration instead of envy. It must be protected and strengthened for the sake of our self-realization, for a fairer society, and for the poor and vulnerable—not just because it is the best system to make us richer, but because it is the most moral system that allows us to flourish as people.

# 2

# A SYSTEM THAT ALLOWS US
# TO EARN OUR SUCCESS

When I was a college professor, I used to teach a course called "Social Entrepreneurship" for students studying nonprofit management. Every year, graduates would ask me for career advice. For many, the choice was between trying to start their own nonprofits and landing a safe job in the management of an existing nonprofit. I told them honestly that they were in for a lot of poverty if they started their own enterprise, but generally advised them to go for it anyway. I knew they would be much happier if they did.

Entrepreneurs of all types rate their well-being higher than any other professional group in America, according to years of polling by the Gallup organization.[1] Why are they so happy? It's not because they're making more money than everyone else; they aren't. According to the employment website careerbuilder.com in 2011, small business owners actually make 19 percent *less* money per year than government managers (and that's ignoring the huge benefits advantage that government workers have over their private-sector counterparts).[2] Nor are entrepreneurs happy because they're working less than other people. Forty-nine percent of the self-employed clock more than forty-four hours per week, versus 39 percent of all workers.[3]

So entrepreneurs work more and make less money than others. But they're happier people. What's their secret? In this chapter, I'll answer this question. It turns out to be the secret to everyone's happiness as well, regardless of whether or not they run their own businesses. I'll offer proof that money itself brings little joy to life, but that the free enterprise system brings what all people truly crave: *earned success*. That is what I believe the Founders meant by the pursuit of happiness.

THESE DAYS, many scholars around the world are studying happiness. It may sound like a squishy topic, but it turns out there is a lot of good evidence on who is happy and who isn't.

We'll look at that in a minute. But first, let's discuss what people *think* will make them happy. At one point, I explored this question, albeit informally. I asked everybody I met—on planes, at parties, wherever—what was the one thing that would make them happier that very day. Some of the responses were funny; a few of them were unprintable.

A surprising number of people mentioned something about money. I say "surprising," because we're all supposed to know that money doesn't buy happiness. Yet a lot of people, including those who are financially comfortable, feel that a little more money would improve their happiness. Is this true? The answer, according to the research on the subject, is not so simple.

One study on money and happiness examines different countries. Are citizens in rich countries happier than those in poorer countries, on average? In 1974, University of Pennsylvania economist Richard Easterlin studied this question and concluded that people in rich countries are generally *not* happier than people in poorer ones.[4] The exceptions to this rule are desperately poor nations in areas like sub-Saharan Africa that are characterized by starvation and disease. But for countries above the level of subsistence—and especially rich, developed countries—money brings little extra happiness. This finding is known as the Easterlin Paradox.[5]

Looking at data for the United States over several decades, then, we shouldn't be too shocked to see that people have gotten a lot richer, but not much happier, on average. In 1972, about 30 percent of Americans told the General Social Survey they were very happy. The average American at that time earned about $25,000 a year, in 2004 dollars. By 2004, the average income had increased to $38,000 (a 50 percent increase in real income).[6] All income groups, from rich to poor, saw substantial income increases. Yet the percentage of very happy Americans stayed virtually unchanged, at 31 percent.

The story is the same in other developed countries. In Japan, real average income was six times higher in 1991 than in 1958. During the post–World War II period, Japan converted at historically unprecedented speed from a poor nation into one of the world's richest. Yet average Japanese happiness didn't change at all over this period.[7]

Maybe the problem is that these increases in average income are too gradual to stimulate happiness. It makes sense to me that three percent income increases, year after year, wouldn't give people a big reason to say they are happier about their lives. But perhaps sudden, huge income increases would do the trick. After all, that's what people think when they imagine getting rich overnight.

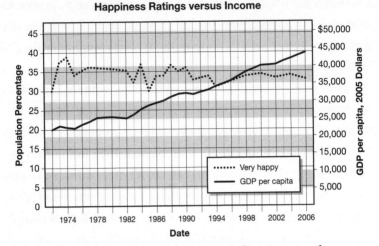

**Figure 2.1.** *While average income in America has risen over the decades, average happiness has not. (Source: James A. Davis, Tom W. Smith, and Peter V. Marsden, General Social Surveys, 1972–2004 [Storrs, Conn.: The Roper Center for Public Opinion Research, University of Connecticut, 2004].)*

Have you ever played the party game where people say what they would do if they won the lottery? The answers are usually predictable, but provide a bit of insight into each person's character and dreams. Some people say they'd travel more or change jobs; others say they would buy things. When men are trying to impress women, they sometimes say, "I'd start a foundation." (Sure they would.)

Whatever they want to do with the money, people always say *good* things would result if they hit the lottery and that their lives would get better. I've never heard anybody say, "If I won the jackpot, I'd make some horrible life choices including marrying somebody who doesn't love me. Next, I'd buy a bunch of things I don't really want. Then, I'd start an ugly alcoholic downward spiral."

But, in fact, the latter scenario is closer to what actually happens when people hit the jackpot. A study by researchers at the

University of Michigan looked at major lottery winners, people who won millions and millions of dollars all at once.[8] The researchers wanted to see how much happier the winners were after they had struck it rich.

The results were depressing. While the winners experienced an immediate happiness boost right after winning, it didn't last. Within a few months, their happiness levels receded to where they had been before winning. As time passed, they found they were actually worse off in happiness than before they had won. The novelty of buying new things wore off. Meanwhile, the small, simple things in life (such as talking to friends or going for a walk) were less pleasurable than they had been in the old days.

One reason money doesn't buy happiness is that people adapt to new economic circumstances incredibly quickly. Maybe you've noticed that you get the most enjoyment from a pay raise the day you find out about it, even more than when you get to spend it, and much more than you will a year after it has become a regular part of your paycheck. Economic gains and losses give pleasure or pain when they happen, but the effect rapidly wears off. People are excellent at perceiving changes to their surroundings or circumstances; they're not so good at sustaining any special sensation from the status quo.

Getting richer is like speeding up a treadmill: There's more activity, but you never get any closer to a goal. According to Adam Smith, a great believer in the benefits of people pursuing economic interests for personal satisfaction, "the mind of every man, in a longer or shorter time, returns to its natural and usual state of tranquility. In prosperity, after a certain time, it falls back to that state; in adversity, after a certain time, it rises up to it."[9] Economists refer to the tendency to adapt as the "hedonic treadmill" and have demonstrated how it works in experiments.

In 1978, economists from the University of Connecticut presented a group of adults in a national sample with a list of twenty-four big-ticket consumer items, such as a car, a house, international travel, a swimming pool, and so on. The economists asked how many of these items the participants currently possessed. They also asked, "When you think of the good life—the life you'd like to have—which of the things on this list, if any, are part of the good life as far as you are personally concerned?"[10] Virtually everybody said that the good life required more things than they currently possessed. Among the people between thirty and forty-four years old, the average number of items owned was 2.5. Their ideal number was 4.3.[11]

The same people were interviewed sixteen years later, in 1994, and were presented with the same list. Naturally, most people had more items; the former thirty- to forty-four-year-olds (now forty-five to fifty-nine-year-olds) had 3.2 items on the list. But had they reached the good life? Of course not. Their requirements had now shifted to 5.4 items.[12] In other words, after sixteen years and lots of work, the good life was just as far off as it had always been. The more stuff people have, the more they want.

IF NOT MONEY, then what do people really crave? The answer is *earned success*, the ability to create value with your life or in the lives of others. It does not come from a lottery check or an inheritance. It doesn't even mean earning a lot of money, given all the blissfully happy social entrepreneurs I've met who are basically living on ramen noodles and tap water.

To earn your success is to define and pursue your happiness as you see fit. It's the freedom to be an individual and to delineate your life's "profit" however you want. For some, this profit is measured in money. But for many, profit is measured in making beautiful art, saving people's souls, or pulling kids out of poverty.

Earned success is what the Founders were talking about in the Declaration of Independence. Charlatans and scoundrels promise happiness. The "Ministry of Plenty" in George Orwell's *1984* promised "our new, happy life."[13] Soviet propaganda called Josef Stalin—on his way to murdering tens of millions—the "Constructor of Happiness."[14] The Founders didn't guarantee happiness. They didn't even say people have the "right to happiness." They said they have the right to *pursue* happiness.

The Founders knew that the role of a moral government is to create the conditions of liberty and opportunity so that each of us can define success as we see fit and then work with all our might to attain it. Their visionary insight was that allowing us to *earn our success* is precisely what gives each of us the best chance at achieving real happiness.

Modern evidence shows that the Founders were absolutely correct. The General Social Survey reveals that people who say they feel "very successful" or "completely successful" in their work lives are twice as likely to say they are very happy about their lives than people who feel "somewhat successful." And it doesn't matter if they earn more or less income; the differences persist.[15]

This finding shows up in survey after survey. A 2001 survey conducted by researchers at Ohio State University found that people who said they did not feel responsible for their own successes spent about 25 percent more time feeling sad than those who said they felt they *were* responsible.[16] This was true whether they were materially prosperous or not.

Here's what all this means to you and me: If I make $50,000 a year and feel I have earned my own success, I'm probably going to be happier than a billionaire who inherits his wealth and *doesn't* feel he's earned his success. Let me define my own success and earn my own way, and then I'll flourish. But take away my ability or incentive to earn my success, and I'll be miserable. If I'm not actually poor, it doesn't matter how many material things I'm given. It doesn't matter how much I receive in government services. I will not be able to achieve what America's Founders said is my "unalienable right" to pursue.


MAYBE YOU AGREE with me here; it's earned success, not money that we want, and that brings us true happiness. It shouldn't be a problem to close the budget gap by taxing people more, because taking away their money won't take away their happiness, right?

Not so fast, Taxman. While it is earned success that really matters, people are nevertheless wired to "keep score." Take away the scoreboard, and they don't play hard (or enjoy the game). This is true in all areas of life. I like to watch professional football because it is interesting and fun, not just to see my beloved Seahawks win. But if they took away the scoreboard and I didn't know who won, I would probably lose interest.

Just for fun, find a Marxist college professor—who scoffs at the idea that people work less if they lose the incentive of money—how he would feel if his name were not put on any of the academic articles he published. Instead the articles would be published under the name of another academic who needed the recognition more than he did. After all, he would still have the satisfaction of having written the articles. Why shouldn't that be enough? His completely reasonable response would be that he *earned* the right to have his name on those articles, and denying him that measure of earned success is viciously unfair. Exactly.

Joseph Schumpeter, often called the godfather of modern entrepreneurship, said of entrepreneurs, "The financial result is a secondary consideration." It is, however, "an index of success and . . . a symptom of victory."[17] Money is the index of success—an imperfect one at that—not success itself. Nonetheless, people still need that index.

Of late, many entrepreneurs have spoken eloquently on this issue. Take BET (Black Entertainment Television) founder Robert Johnson, for example. In reaction to President Obama's calls to raise taxes on "millionaires and billionaires," Johnson said,

> I grew up in a family of 10 kids, first one to go to college, and I've earned my success. I've earned my right to fly private if I choose to do so. And by attacking me it is not going to convince me that I should take a bigger hit because I happen to be wealthy. . . . It doesn't mean that I am a bad guy. . . . I went into business to create jobs and opportunity, create opportunity, create value for myself and my investors. And that's what the president should be praising.[18]

Johnson is not a conservative. In fact, he has donated hundreds of thousands of dollars to Democratic candidates and causes. But he has discovered the key to American happiness. He wants to live in an America where hard work and success are rewarded, and the *measures* of hard work and success are protected.

Think about your own life and work—the jobs you've enjoyed and the jobs you haven't. Have you ever quit a job because, no matter how hard you worked and how clever you were, your material rewards had stalled? Consider this: 70 percent of people who say their chances for promotion are good are "very satisfied" with their jobs, versus just 42 percent who say their chances for promotion are not good. To be happy, people need clear paths to success and the ability to measure and keep rewards.[19]

IT IS FAIR AND RIGHT for people to want to keep the measures of their earned success. But it is easy to become focused *only* on money as a measure of success. This is a dangerous mistake.

People do awful things for money, including unearned money, which the evidence shows brings zero (or even negative) happiness. They fight over inheritances; they steal from others; they gamble compulsively. How can it be that even many rich people still haven't figured out that earned success—not money—is the correct object of their desires?

The short answer is that people screw up. Or, as social scientists prefer to put it, people commit an "epistemic error." People mistake what they want for the *measure* of what they want. I want a blood pressure reading of 120/80, but that is nothing more than an indicator of the force of my blood running through my arteries; it is not heart health itself. For years, I tried to explain to my university students, who always worried a lot about their grades, that their grade point average was only a rough measure of wisdom. (Somehow this brought them no comfort.)

In economic life, earned success itself is messy and hard to define. Money is a neat and convenient measure of it, so people focus on money instead. The common word for that kind of epistemic error is *materialism*, and it leads to misery. As the Roman poet Persius said, "Oh, what void there is in things."

Social scientists have repeatedly proven Persius right. In 2011, a group of psychologists at several American universities found that kids who were most attached to material objects were the least grateful for the blessings in their lives, most envious of others, and enjoyed their activities outside of school least. Materialistic kids are unhappy kids.[20]

But materialism's curse is most brutal later in life, especially for men. One of the common findings in studies of happiness is that there is a distinct low point in men's happiness in their mid-forties. (Women don't have this dip.) Using the General Social Survey data from 2004, I have found that the happiness nadir occurs right around age forty-five for the average American male, even after correcting for income, education, race, religion, and politics.[21]

So what's going on at age 45—the clichéd male midlife crisis? Psychologists have explanations that revolve around marriage and family. They basically say that the problem for men at age forty-five is that wives have pretty much figured out their husbands are boring. In addition, there is probably at least one sullen teenager living at home.

But there's an economic explanation, too. When men start their careers, earned success and money track together pretty well. They get better jobs, win promotions, make more money, acquire more responsibility, and live their dreams, year by year. But the roads between money and earned success begin to diverge, so subtly that it is hard to notice at first. Men tend to follow the professional superhighway, the one with the big neon dollar signs. The road to self-realization, the pursuit of happiness, is a little path through the woods that they easily miss.

By forty-five, a lot of guys realize they took the wrong road. They recognize their epistemic error. Some can trace back their steps. Personally, I got lucky and saw fairly early that I was going the wrong way, and went back to find the little path. The trouble is that not all forty-five-year-old guys can retrace their steps (or think they can't) and end up saying, "I *hate* my job, but I have to pay my mortgage."

EARNED SUCCESS has a flip side: learned helplessness. This term was coined by the social psychologist Martin Seligman at the University of Pennsylvania.[22] Learned helplessness is a state in which, if rewards and punishments are not tied to merit, people simply give up and stop trying to succeed.

Seligman examined learned helplessness in experiments on both animals and humans. In one study, he found that dogs subjected to inescapable and arbitrary electric shocks had greater difficulty taking steps to escape pain from predictable sources than dogs that hadn't gotten the arbitrary shocks.[23] Experience taught them that they were powerless to positively influence their circumstances. In later studies, human subjects presented with insoluble problems or exposed to inescapable unpleasant noises subsequently had greater difficulty with ordinary tasks.[24] Their helplessness early on incapacitated them later.

Just as earned success brings happiness, learned helplessness brings unhappiness. As Seligman noted in an interview in the *New York Times*, "We found that even when good things occurred that weren't earned, like nickels coming out of slot machines, it did not increase people's well-being. It produced helplessness. People gave up and became passive."[25]

The implications for the welfare state are too obvious to miss. If the government gives people rewards they did not earn—welfare checks, make-work jobs, or whatever—it will not improve their well-being. Even worse, it will make them helpless.

This is surely why people go to such contortions to act as if their unearned rewards from government were actually earned. In the 1970s, it was common to refer to welfare as a "salary." Today, the easiest way to get yourself shot at a retirement village is to suggest that senior citizens are taking more out of the Social Security system than they ever put in.

As bad as unearned rewards are, unearned punishments are even worse. That is why onerous regulation and punitive taxation are so harmful, and why it is so demoralizing for the general population to learn that we pay taxes to fund public-sector benefits and pensions that, in the case of the federal government, are 61 percent more lavish than equivalent workers receive in the private sector.[26] It is also why it is so discouraging to see tax dollars bail out politically connected banks and car companies.

The message is clear: People thrive when they can earn their success, and they suffer under conditions in which they can't, or are trained not to, succeed. People flourish when they control their lives. When that is taken away from them by the state or corporate cronies, everyone suffers.

FOR THE MAJORITY OF PEOPLE, the most common source of earned success is work.

People need to work. Philosopher Erich Fromm wrote that "only in being productively active can man make sense of his life."[27] This is partly correct; unproductivity is obviously terrible, which is one of the reasons unemployed people have such high depression rates. But being "productively active" is not enough. Slaves are productively active. To earn their success, people have to be more than just productive; they must also choose their own paths and have a chance at finding the work that matches their passions with their talents. That match is what Albert Camus called the "soul" in work. "Without work, all life goes rotten. But when work is soulless, life stifles and dies."[28] I came to understand this—and to appreciate the system that offered a chance to find the soul in my work—through firsthand experience.

I used to have what some considered the best job possible, yet was unhappy. I spent my whole childhood playing music—violin, then piano, and then finally the French horn. From the age of nine, playing the horn was practically all I did. I worked hard, year after year, with hours and hours of practice, rehearsals, lessons, and competitions. I never thought about *whether* I would pursue a career as a musician; it was simply inevitable. I skipped college to go professional, taking a job with a brass quintet. I toured Alaska in February and Arizona in July, and practiced like crazy. After a few years, I won a job playing in a symphony orchestra—the dream of most classical musicians.

My friends in the orchestra thrived on what they were doing and threw themselves into it with abandonment. They would spend their vacations at classical music conventions and heatedly discuss the most esoteric details of the lacquer on their instruments. Try as I might, I lacked such ardor. I loved great music, but found the production of it punitive and exacting, and I knew my job would never change much. My friends had found the soul in their work, but I hadn't found the soul in mine.

So in my late twenties, I hatched a plot to quit. I took a job teaching music during the day, and (without telling anyone but my wife) studied economics at night until I had a bachelor's degree. At age thirty-one, I gave up the horn and started graduate school, planning to become a social scientist and write books. This was a crazy idea for a French horn player. When I called my father to announce my career change, he asked incredulously, "Why do you want to leave music, when it's going so well?" "Because I'm not happy," I told him. He was silent for a moment and then demanded, "What makes *you* so special?"

The fact is, I'm *not* so special. I'm just an American, and I understood instinctively that the genius of our free enterprise system is that it makes it possible for people to reinvent themselves and earn their success.[29] That is why the U.S. has always been a magnet for people from other parts of the world who want to transform their lives. It has created a society of opportunity-seeking strivers who can match their skills and passions—the America our Founders envisioned, and Alexis de Tocqueville marveled at when he said, "What most astonishes me in the United States, is not so much the marvelous grandeur of some undertakings, as the innumerable multitude of small ones."[30]

America's system allowed me to find the work where my soul resides. Today, I feel I earn my success, and my job gives me joy. I now look forward to work, and probably spend twice as much time doing it each week as I ever did during my years in music. I work so much now that someone who doesn't understand the system that matches people with the work they love—a European social democrat, for example—might think I'm a crazed workaholic. As a matter of fact, that's basically the view that Europeans have of most Americans.

Have you ever heard the old expression that Americans live to work and Europeans work to live? It's basically true. Americans work 50 percent more than the Italians, French, and even the Germans.[31]

Why? Some argue that it's because Americans are terrified of losing our jobs; others claim it's due to our quasi-religious work ethic. According to *Time* magazine, "in the puritanical version of Christianity that has always appealed to Americans, religion comes packaged with the stern message that hard work is good for the soul. Modern Europe has avoided so melancholy a lesson."[32]

While that analysis might sound compelling to some people, earned success is a better explanation for Americans' work ethic. Simply put, work in America creates more personal value than it does in other places. Numerous studies have shown that Americans enjoy greater social mobility than Europeans, and becoming successful in one's work can raise social status.[33] In addition, Americans have traditionally been taxed less on their labor income than Europeans, which means harder work is rewarded financially.[34]

Not surprisingly, working makes Americans much happier than it makes Europeans. One economist at the University of Texas-Dallas has used numerous databases to show that Americans outrank Europeans in happiness at high work levels, while the reverse is true at low work levels.[35] Europeans are happiest working thirty-five to thirty-nine hours per week. Americans are happiest working fifty to fifty-nine hours. My own data analysis shows that "very happy" Americans work more hours each week than those who are "pretty happy," who in turn work more hours than people who are "not too happy."[36]

The vast majority of Americans like their jobs. Among adults who worked ten hours a week or more in 2002, 89 percent said they were very satisfied or somewhat satisfied with their jobs.[37] And people with high-paying jobs aren't the only ones who are satisfied. There is no difference between those with below- and above-average incomes: 89 percent are satisfied.[38]

In America, job satisfaction relates to life satisfaction. Among those who say they are very happy in their lives, 95 percent are also satisfied with their jobs. Only 5 percent say they are not satisfied with their work.[39] The evidence also shows that the relationship is causal: job satisfaction actually *increases* life happiness.[40]

Europeans find this notion mind-boggling. When I describe American work habits to my European in-laws, they just shake their heads and make derisive comments about how brainwashed we all are. Even weirder, they think, is our attitude about vacations. When getting to know a European, a typical question is, "Where are you going on vacation this year?" You rarely hear this trivial conversation in America. There is no indication that Americans wish they had more vacation time than they have already. Only 11 percent of American workers say they wish they could spend a lot less time on their jobs.[41]

Am I arguing that Americans are happier than Europeans and that Europeans could be as happy as Americans are, if only they embraced our system? Actually, I'm not. Europeans do reasonably well on happiness indexes. One British study from 2006 compared 128 countries worldwide and concluded that Denmark was the happiest country in the world, even somewhat more so than the United States.[42] Other surveys show that the United States has the edge. But either way, it's clear that Europeans think they're pretty happy.

It is reasonable to assume that Americans and Europeans are different, on average, and are made happy by different things. For most Americans, work in a free enterprise system that matches our skills and talents is essential to happiness, so the European system would be wrong for *us*. Immigrants with "American wiring" come to our shores to work hard and create value. European-style social democracy would make it harder for most Americans—whether they are Americans by birth or by choice—to earn our success and would make us unhappier as a people. We need to resist all efforts to push America in a European direction.


WHEN I DESCRIBE earned success, perhaps I seem to be talking only about the good things in life. After all, flourishing and happiness don't come from pain and suffering, right?

Wrong. According to the great Hindu yogi Paramahansa Yogananda, "the weakling who has refused the conflict, acquiring nothing, has had nothing to renounce. He alone who has striven and won can enrich the world by bestowing the fruits of his victorious experience."[43] Earned success requires sacrifice. And a system that dedicates itself to expunging the challenge and risk from people's lives is immoral.

Whenever you ask entrepreneurs about their success, they spend a great deal of time describing the hardships: early failures and bankruptcies, missed little league games, and endless nights without sleep. They talk about almost losing their homes and the strain all this put on their marriages.

Take Bernie Marcus, founder of The Home Depot, the $60 billion home improvement retail chain. Marcus initially struggled desperately to make the venture work. At the first store's grand opening in 1979, he sent his friends and family into the street to give away $1 bills to lure people into the empty store. The result? "We literally couldn't give the dollar bills away," he recalled.[44] He jokes that his wife wouldn't let him shave during this time, because she didn't want him to be alone with a razor blade.

The legendary investment company founder Charles Schwab is another example. When asked about the incredible success of his $15 billion company, he tells the story about taking out a second mortgage on his home just to make payroll in the early years.[45]

The focus on early failure is funny, when you think about it. If you ask a friend about a vacation to Mexico she clearly enjoyed, she'll talk mostly about how sunny it was and how beautiful the beach was—not so much about how it had increased her chances for melanoma or how the airline lost her luggage. Yet happy, successful entrepreneurs always talk about how much they sacrificed before attaining success.

I asked Bernie Marcus why entrepreneurs always recall the sacrifices when they talk about the path to prosperity. For him, he told me, sacrifices were central to his later earned success. Failure, anxiety, and lean years weren't just necessarily evils; they were lessons to learn and tests to pass. They were the "earned" part of "earned success," and there was no substitute for them. Without sacrifice, either there's no success or, at the very least, it's not earned. Either way, it's no good.

When we hear about successful entrepreneurs, it is always as if they had the Midas touch. You know the story: A pimply college kid cooks up an Internet company during a boring lecture at Harvard, and before lunch, he's a billionaire. But in real life, that's not how it works. Steven Rogers, in *The Entrepreneur's Guide to Finance and Business*, reports that the average entrepreneur fails 3.8 times before succeeding.[46] According to careerbuilder.com, the average small-business owner earns $44,576 per year in personal income, hardly a fortune, and a lot less than the average civil servant.[47]

Entrepreneurs aren't generally rich, and they fail a lot. When they sacrifice, they are learning and improving, exactly what they need to do to earn their success through their merits. Every sacrifice and failure makes them smarter and better, showing them that they're not getting anything for free. When success ultimately comes, they wouldn't trade away the earlier sacrifice for anything, even if they felt wretched at the time.

Experimental psychologists have shown in novel ways the link between the ability to sacrifice and success. In one famous study from 1972, Stanford psychologist Walter Mischel concocted an experiment involving young children and a bag of marshmallows. A researcher would put a marshmallow on the table and tell the child he was leaving the room for a little while. He told the child that if he or she could refrain from eating the marshmallow until the researcher came back fifteen minutes later, the child would get another one as a reward.[48]

It sounds easy, but it wasn't. About two-thirds of the kids failed the experiment. Some gave up immediately and gobbled up the marshmallow as soon as the researcher walked out. Videotape shows other kids in agony, trying to discipline themselves to get the sweet reward—some even banging their little heads on the table.

But the most interesting results from that study came years later. Researchers followed up on the kids in the study to see how their lives were turning out. What was the difference between the kids who waited, and the kids who didn't? The kids who took the marshmallow immediately had average SAT scores 210 points lower than the kids who refrained. They dropped out of college at higher rates, made far less money, were more likely to go to jail, and suffered from more drug and alcohol problems.[49]

So let's return to public policy as it relates to sacrifice. The welfare state exists, in no small part, to shove the marshmallows into our mouths. It gets rid of sacrifice. It smoothes out our economic lives and protects us from unpleasant downsides. The welfare state—including not just those who receive welfare checks but everyone else who relies on the state to bail them out as well—protects people from the vicissitudes of life.

For instance, during the current mortgage crisis, politicians justified bailing out mortgage holders by blaming banks for selling mortgages to people who couldn't afford them. In some cases, this was undoubtedly true. But according to researchers at the National Bureau of Economic Research, about a quarter of the people who defaulted on their mortgages during the economic crisis did so "strategically"—that is, they could afford to pay but chose not to.[50] Yet by law, they could walk away from their mortgages without losing any of their other personal property. Thousands were bailed out with tax money.

The National Flood Insurance Program is another glaring example of how the federal government protects citizens from the consequences of the risks they take. For less than $600 per year—far below what any private insurance company would charge in this market—the program insures homeowners who choose to build houses in flood plains, some of the riskiest real estate in America.[51] The program is currently $19 billion in debt as a result of taking on risks that the homeowners themselves should assume if they want to live in disaster-prone areas.

The most obvious example of the federal government protecting citizens from the consequences of their actions is the massive bailouts of banks, failed corporations, and government-sponsored enterprises (GSEs) Fannie Mae and Freddie Mac in 2008 and 2009. The federal government made an open-ended commitment to Fannie and Freddie, the failed Washington, D.C., giants that sparked the housing crisis and recession. As of July 2011, this has cost taxpayers $317 billion, according to the Congressional Budget Office.[52] Similarly, when the private market deemed Chrysler and General Motors too uncompetitive to succeed, the government handed these companies $80 billion in taxpayer money.[53]

Thus, Americans, who boast to the world about independence and resourcefulness, become infantilized. We see more and more preposterous examples of the attitudes this creates. During the 2011 Occupy Wall Street protests in New York, a reporter interviewed a young man holding a sign that read, "Throw me a bone, pay my tuition." When asked why he thought the government should pay his college tuition, his answer was, "Because it's what I want."[54] During the 2008 presidential campaign, a Florida woman was asked in an interview why she was supporting Barack Obama for president. If he is elected, she told the interviewer, "I won't have to worry about putting gas in my car. I won't have to worry about paying my mortgage. . . . If I help him, he's going to help me."[55]

People who avail themselves of welfare and bailouts are not bad or stupid. They are just human. No one is eager to sacrifice all that much. I bet that many entrepreneurs who say they now cherish their sacrifices would (at the time) have welcomed faster, easier success. But if people are given a way out of every crisis and challenge, they are both less likely to succeed in the long term and less likely to enjoy any success that they acquire because it's unearned. Bailouts that do more than provide a minimum standard of living—whether mortgage relief or a billion-dollar bank bailout—teach the wrong lessons and lead people to learned helplessness.

INSTEAD OF offering more data, studies, and experiments that show how redistributive ways are making the pursuit of happiness harder by penalizing earned success and enabling learned helplessness, here is a poem I like entitled, "Tame Duck," published in 1929 in a newsletter from the Milwaukee Co-operative Milk Producers.[56] For me it describes, in an amusing way, the lives we face if we turn our backs on American free enterprise.

> There are two tame ducks in our backyard,
> Dabbling in mud and trying hard
> To get their share, and maybe more
> of the overflowing barnyard store.
> They're fairly content with the task they're at
> Of eating and sleeping and getting fat.
> But whenever the free wild ducks go by
> In a long line streaming down the sky,

They cock a quizzical, puzzled eye
And flap their wings and try to fly.
I think my soul is a tame old duck
Dabbling around in barnyard muck,
Fat and lazy, with useless wings,
But at times, when the north wind sings
And the wild ones hurtle overhead
It remembers something lost and dead,
And cocks a wary, bewildered eye
And makes a feeble attempt to fly.
It's fairly content with the state it's in
But it isn't the duck that it might have been!

EARNED SUCCESS, not materialism and government redistribution, is the way to understand the Founders' moral promise of the pursuit of happiness in America today. The free enterprise system allows the most people to earn their success, going far beyond the benefits of mere money. Free enterprise is therefore not an economic imperative; it is a moral imperative.

Free enterprise requires the existence of a level playing field, though. Some may say that the concept of earned success rings hollow because America is not a *fair society*. Capitalism, we hear, simply rewards a privileged few.

We need to deal with these claims about fairness. So that is the next subject.

# 3

# A System That Is Fair

Imagine a typical family—a mom, a dad, and three young children. The kids have been asking mom and dad to adopt a dog, but the parents are resistant. Dad, in particular, objects. Dogs are dirty, he argues. They mess up the house. And you have to walk them all the time.

But the kids are persistent and pretty soon they win over mom. Dad quickly caves in front of this new coalition. They adopt a puppy from the pound and name her Muffin.

Dad is proved wrong. Muffin turns out to be a *great* dog: friendly, intelligent, and wonderful with the kids. Everyone loves her, especially dad. They all laugh at how he didn't want to get her in the first place.

A couple of years pass. One day, the family's youngest child accidentally leaves the front door open. Muffin sees a squirrel in the neighbor's yard and takes off in hot pursuit. She darts into the street and is hit by a speeding car. She dies on the spot in front of the whole family.

Everyone is understandably heartbroken. The kids are crying, mom is crying, and even dad tears up. Lovingly, they pick up Muffin's lifeless body and bring her in the house. After a short family discussion, they come to a decision about what to do next.

*They decide to cook and eat Muffin.*

IF YOU ARE LIKE ME—and everyone else I know—you're either laughing or shaking your head in disgust. That ending is just wrong. (Try the story at your next dinner party and see!) Is eating the dog—bizarre to be sure—morally okay? Just about everyone will say, "Of course not." But why not? Nobody is physically harmed by the act, least of all the dead dog. It's legal, and people eat animals all the time. Still, people say, it's just *wrong*.

This story is liberally adapted from the work of Jonathan Haidt, a social psychologist at the University of Virginia and the world's leading expert on the science of morality. Haidt and his co-authors have conducted a string of experiments in which they present human subjects with situations about which they have an immediate and overwhelming moral reaction, but one that they cannot justify rationally for minutes, hours, or sometimes ever.[1] (The dog story is one of the tamer tales.) Haidt explains that when people are confronted with an emotionally evocative situation like the one in the story about the dog, their intuitive minds kick into gear and send their reasoning minds out on a mission: find a rational justification for my moral judgment! Generally what people eventually come up with (for example, "In our society, it is not alright to eat your pets") simply justifies their initial moral predilections. You are unlikely to persuade people based on logic and reason that their initial moral judgment was wrong.

Public policy debates are similar: People have very quick moral reactions and respond strongly to moral appeals. Once they are leaning morally in one direction, it's extremely difficult to push them the other way using logic and evidence. Imagine you are debating someone about the virtues of free enterprise. You can be ready with all the PowerPoint charts in the world about the economic efficiency of the capitalist economy, but the moment your interlocutor says, "Capitalism is unfair to the poor!" you've lost the debate. You might as well try to convince somebody to eat his dog.

Right now, that's the situation in which free enterprise advocates find themselves. From the Occupy Wall Street Movement to more moderate liberal politicians, income inequality has become the bogeyman on the basis of nothing more than the moral claim that the free enterprise system is unfair because it rewards some people so much more than others. They ask how a few enjoy billions of dollars when so many others have less. They say it's morally repugnant.

It does not matter very much if this kind of fairness claim is logically dubious. A materialistic rejoinder about economic growth and balanced budgets will not persuade the American public to turn away from big government policies. Only a moral rejoinder about the *fairness* of rewarding merit through free enterprise will carry the day.

ALTHOUGH CURMUDGEONS will argue that America has become a land of moral relativism, Americans do, in fact, share a common set of beliefs about what is right and wrong.

Through extensive surveys, Haidt (of the dog-eating experiment) has established what these beliefs are. He has asked people indirect moral questions such as, "How much money would it take to get you to accept a plasma screen television that a friend of yours wants to give you? You know that your friend got the television a year ago when the company that made it sent it to him by mistake and at no cost to him." Using sophisticated statistical techniques, Haidt distilled the answers to his questions and found that in America and around the world, fairness is a universally shared moral value.

Except for sociopaths, people crave fairness and naturally try to act fairly. This trait appears to be wired in from the youngest ages. Psychologists have studied this in a number of creative ways. For example, two Swedish researchers showed several dozen four-and-a-half year-olds a puppet show in which one puppet was struggling to complete a task. The puppet was helped by another but violently hindered by a third. Afterward, the researchers asked the kids to distribute an odd number of toys between the helper and the hinderer. They almost always favored the helping puppet and justified this decision in terms of fairness.[2]

In another study, social psychologists at the University of Toronto asked students to predict how much they would cheat on a simple math test in order to get a small prize. The average student said he would cheat on almost one-third of the questions. When confronted with the actual ability to do so though—with no repercussions—the participants actually had a physically negative reaction: the researchers found that the participants' hearts pounded, their palms sweated, and they became short of breath. The students' bodies reacted adversely to the immorality of taking the test unfairly, and they cheated far less than anticipated.[3]

A commitment to the idea of fairness seems to be bred to the bone. The problem is that the definition of "fairness" is ambiguous. We see this ambiguity around us constantly. For example, I have three kids, and they fight a lot. If there's one cookie left, they will inevitably make multiple claims on it. The conflict goes something like this:

"I want the last cookie!"

"No, I should get it!"

"But that's not fair—you already had two, and I had only one!"

"Yes, but I helped Mom make them!"

At this point, I generally intervene and eat the cookie. (Being a dad has its privileges.) But the point is that the kids are arguing over the definition of fairness, not just a cookie. One thinks "fair" means "equal." The other thinks "fair" means "earned."

This is just like many policy arguments. Some people argue that the income structure and tax code aren't fair, because they leave the rich with so much more money than the poor, while social programs are, as administration officials commonly say, "desperately underfunded."[4] Others disagree, arguing that taking resources away from people who earned them honestly, just to equalize outcomes, is unfair.

Here, in short, are the two definitions of fairness in American economic life today.[5]

Definition one: *Redistributive fairness.* It is fair to equalize rewards. Inequality is inherently unfair.

Definition two: *Meritocratic fairness.* Fairness means matching reward to merit. Forced equality is inherently unfair.

Many progressive politicians publicly subscribe to the first definition. For example, former House Speaker Nancy Pelosi has complained publicly that the United States is becoming a nation in which "wealthy people continue to get wealthier" at the expense of the less fortunate. Why is this a problem? "It's all about fairness in our country," she says.[6] The president of the United States has proposed tax increases on families earning more than $250,000 a year as part of his attempts to get "more fairness" in the tax code.[7]

Many Americans—perhaps you—disagree with the claim that fairness requires less income inequality. They think that higher taxes may be necessary for the country—or not. But either way, redistribution does not make society "fairer." That's because they prefer the second definition.

The fact that there is more than one definition of fairness led the great Nobel laureate economist Milton Friedman to write that "'fairness' is not an objectively determined concept. 'Fairness,' like 'needs,' is in the eye of the beholder."[8] Many economists have taken this to mean that people should dismiss the whole concept of fairness and ignore it as hopelessly subjective, even childish, like the argument between my kids.

This is a mistake. To dismiss fairness is like dismissing *love*: a difficult phenomenon to identify quantitatively, but a central facet of life and hugely important to nearly everybody.

THE REAL QUESTION is not *whether* fairness matters—it does—but *which definition is correct for public policy*. Is it equal outcomes, rewarding merit, or something in between? Social scientists over the years have developed experiments and surveys that help answer this question.

One fairness experiment is called an "ultimatum game." Two subjects who don't know each other—imagine they're you and me—are asked to split a certain amount of money—say, $10. I am given the $10 and am instructed to choose how much to offer you. I offer you $3 and keep $7. Next, you are told to accept or reject the offer. If you accept, we both keep the respective amounts. If you reject the offer, we both walk away empty-handed.

Classical economic theory predicts that you should accept any positive offer I make. If I offer you a penny and propose to keep $9.99, you'll take it because it's better than getting nothing, according to the theory.

But, of course, that's wrong. If the offer seems too unfair, you'll walk away out of spite and punish me for my selfishness. In the United States, games like this have an average offer of about $4. People reject the offer between 9 and 17 percent of the time.[9]

When the ultimatum game is played in various other countries, the results differ significantly. Researchers observed the highest offers in Paraguay, where good-hearted Paraguayans offered grateful partners a bit more than half, on average. They observed that the lowest offers were in Spain, about $2.50, on average. Not coincidentally, Spain has the highest offer-rejection rate, approaching 30 percent. (According to my Spanish wife, this explains some of the problems in doing business in Spain.)

Just for fun, I tried the ultimatum game using my three kids as subjects. My two sons (ages eleven and thirteen) and my daughter (age eight) each got to play on both sides of the game with the other two, using ten pieces of candy in each round.[10] The big winner was my daughter.[11] She made generous offers to my sons, got generous offers in return, and suffered no rejections. She ended up with eighteen pieces of candy. My sons made miserly offers to each other, which each summarily rejected with great prejudice. Their haul of eleven pieces each came entirely from good trade relations with their little sister.

In the ultimatum game, merit is not part of the experiment. Nobody earns the resources they are bargaining over. You walk into the room, and somebody gives you ten bucks (or ten pieces of candy). That's it. Under these circumstances, participants find it unfair to try to keep too much. That's why they are willing to reject offers in order to punish others, even when it means personal sacrifice. Fairness matters to people, even in little experiments.

When merit comes into the mix, however, people's perceptions change a lot. If you *earn* what you have, most people think you have a right to keep it, even if others end up with less.

There are no ultimatum games using earned income, but there are surveys that show the same thing. For example, in 2006, the World Values Survey asked a large sample of Americans to consider this scenario:

> Imagine two secretaries, of the same age, doing
> practically the same job. One finds out that the other
> earns considerably more than she does. The better
> paid secretary, however, is quicker, more efficient
> and more reliable at her job.[12]

Then the survey asked, "Is it fair or not fair that one secretary is paid more than the other?" To this question, 88.6 percent answered that it was fair to pay the better secretary more, while 11.4 percent said it was unfair.

So which is the "right" definition for American public policy: redistributive fairness or meritocratic fairness? The answer is, "it depends." When people do not perceive resources to have been earned (as in the ultimatum game), they think it fair that the resources be split somewhat evenly. When merit is involved (as in the case of the two secretaries), people believe that unequal rewards are fairer than equal rewards.

When I was a university professor, I used to make this point to my economics students in an unorthodox way. There was always a lot of class discussion about how society should distribute income. Many of the students were politically progressive, and I probably heard them say a thousand times that it is "not fair" the rich in America have so much more than the poor. *Fairness* was their rationale for income redistribution.

So I set up a thought experiment. Halfway through the course, I could see big differences between students who were working hard and those who weren't. The hard workers got lots of points on their tests and quizzes; their less motivated friends didn't. We all knew that the students with the highest point totals were working harder than the others. They might have been a bit brighter or already knew more about economics, but the *real* difference was how much they were studying.

I proposed that the class take a quarter of the points earned by the top half of the class and pass them on to the students in the lower half of the class. The students were in unanimous agreement that this was a stupid idea. Redistributing points earned on the basis of hard work and merit, simply so that students who didn't study could get a higher grade, would be completely unfair. Even students at the bottom thought the scheme was idiotic.

I didn't have to spell out my point. Beyond providing for essential services and a minimum safety net, redistributing earned income just to get more equality is not fair.

If income were handed out purely arbitrarily, then most of us would viscerally agree that the money should be redistributed in a more-or-less equal way. But income is not handed out to people purely arbitrarily. Most of us believe that even if the system is imperfect, we earn our success through hard work and initiative—in a word, through *merit*. Most of us understand that some redistribution is necessary to pay for a functioning government. But relatively few believe that the resources people earn should be redistributed to help equalize outcomes.

THE UNITED STATES was founded on the ideals of meritocratic fairness. Alexis de Tocqueville wrote that Americans are "contemptuous of the theory of permanent equality of wealth."[13] Thomas Jefferson famously said it in this way:

> To take from one, because it is thought his own industry and that of his fathers has acquired too much, in order to spare to others, who, or whose fathers, have not exercised equal industry and skill, is to violate arbitrarily the first principle of association, the guarantee to everyone the free exercise of his industry and the fruits acquired by it.[14]

The views of Tocqueville and Jefferson follow an ancient truth: that to take resources from those who legitimately earn them and give them to another who does not is not fair. If it is voluntary, it is charitable. But if it is coerced, it is *un*fair. Aristotle put it best: "The worst form of inequality is to try to make unequal things equal."

Following in the footsteps of the Founders, Americans prefer rewarding merit over redistribution. Public opinion studies show this, such as the one about the two secretaries. Still, a lot was left to the imagination in the story of those two secretaries. Did they both have access to a good education? Had both received equiva-lent training for the job? For their unequal salaries to translate into a fair economic system, both the secretaries needed the opportu-nity to develop their abilities. It's not so fair, for example, if the less effective secretary couldn't go to school and didn't know how to read.

If individual opportunity is a sham—if the system is fixed and some people get the breaks only by virtue of luck or birth or skin color—then inequality isn't fair at all. We should redistribute wealth the same way we should redistribute unearned candy.[15] But if America is an opportunity society—if, in fact, people have the chance to work harder, get more education, and innovate—then rewarding merit is fair, and for some people to make more money than others is good and just.

The real question, then, is whether America is an opportunity society. If it is, then inequality is fair. If it isn't, then inequality isn't fair.

According to the evidence, the United States is an opportunity society, even if an imperfect one. One way to show this is by looking at whether people can and do get ahead economically. University of Michigan-Flint economist Mark Perry has analyzed data from the Federal Reserve Bank of Minneapolis to see whether Americans are mobile between income classes. He asked the ques-tions, "If you're poor in America, does this mean you'll stay poor? And if you're rich, are you set for life?"[16]

The answer to both questions was a resounding no. The poor can and do rise in America, according to Perry's research, and the rich can and do fall. He shows that 44 percent of households in the bottom income quintile (the lowest 20 percent of earners) in 2001 had moved to a higher quintile by 2007. During the same period, 34 percent in the highest quintile in 2001 moved to a lower

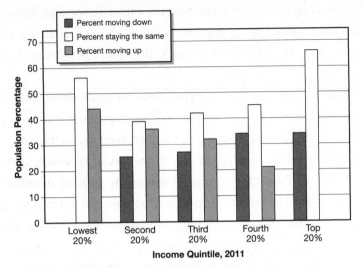

**Figure 3.1.** *Starting out poor or rich in America is no guarantee of staying that way. (Source: Mark Perry, "Income Mobility in the Dynamic U.S. Economy," 29 March 2011,* The Enterprise Blog, *http://blog.american.com/2011/03/income-mobility-in-the-dynamic -u-s-economy/.)*

quintile by 2007. In other words, if you are poor, the chances are about one in two that you'll be doing better within a few years. If you are at the top, the chances are about one in three that you won't stay there very long.

Perry's results are typical. Economists at Urban Institute (a center-left think tank) conducted a large survey of the studies on income mobility in America, concluding that "mobility is significant and has remained stable over time."[17] Using the University of Michigan's Panel Study of Income Dynamics—the most comprehensive nonpartisan data source tracking people and their incomes over the decades—economists have found that the likelihood of escaping the bottom quintile in a ten-year period is 44 percent.[18] Another study using the same data found that the escape rate over five years is 38 percent.[19]

Not everybody rises from poverty, but millions and millions do. This means real people in America are experiencing real opportunity, all the time. For them, the American Dream is no illusion.

I am not arguing that everybody has an equal chance to rise. A lot of people are stuck at the bottom, especially if they have gotten an inadequate education, or have been on welfare and if their parents were on welfare, too.[20] The Great Recession that is continuing as I write has seriously harmed the mobility of millions of hard-working people thrown out of work or unable to get ahead. But the data simply do not support the idea that the deck is hopelessly stacked against the poor.

Given the facts, it's hardly a surprise to find that huge majorities of Americans believe the U.S. is an opportunity society. In 2005, when Syracuse University researchers asked a cross-section of Americans, "Do you think everyone in American society has an opportunity to succeed, most do, or do only some have this opportunity?" 71.3 percent responded that everyone or most people have an opportunity to succeed.[21]

This belief has persisted for many years, probably since the founding of the United States (although there is no data going back that far). The General Social Survey has asked a large sample of Americans since 1973 to answer this question: "Some people say that people get ahead by their own hard work, others say that lucky breaks or help from other people are more important. Which do you think is most important?" For forty years, between 60 and 70 percent of Americans have said "hard work," while never more than 16 percent have said "lucky breaks."[22]

This faith in the effectiveness of hard work is distinctly American. In the World Values Survey conducted between 2005 and 2007, researchers asked people in fifty-four countries whether hard work brings success or whether success is more a matter of luck and connections. Americans were more likely than people in other developed countries to say success comes from hard work; for example, they were more than twice as likely as the French to give this response.[23] This may be why many believe America is—for now—an aspirational society, while Europe is more animated by envy. The singer Bono summed it up evocatively: "In Ireland people have an interesting attitude to success; they look down on it. In America, you look up at . . . the mansion on the hill and say, 'One day . . . that could be me.' In Ireland, they look up at the mansion on the hill and go, 'One day I'm gonna get that bastard.'"[24]

Most Americans believe the U.S. is an opportunity society—but not all do. The biggest difference on this score is political ideology. According to the Syracuse University data, the people least likely to say they believe in the opportunity society today are political progressives. Liberals, including successful liberals, believe less than conservatives—even poorer conservatives—that economic mobility is actually possible in America. Forty-eight percent of lower-income conservatives believe there's a lot of upward income mobility in America, versus 26 percent of upper-income liberals. And 90 percent of the poorer—but optimistic—conservatives said that hard work and perseverance could overcome disadvantage, versus just 65 percent of richer liberals.[25]

For now, the optimistic view is the mainstream view, though, given that seven in ten Americans still believe in abundant opportunity. This is not very surprising, I suppose; it may even be in our genes. Had our ancestors not believed in the correlation between hard work and success, most of us wouldn't even be here. If you're descended from immigrants (and most of us are), ask yourself why your ancestors came here. I am confident they didn't come to America in search of a stronger system of government income redistribution. Letters from my own great-grandparents who emigrated from Denmark suggest they came to America to earn their success. They wanted to start a farm, and to be rewarded if they worked hard. A system without opportunity, where merit was not rewarded, was what they were escaping *from* in Europe.

Generation after generation of immigrants came to America for the same reasons that my family did.[26] Abraham Lincoln promised, "When one starts poor, as most do in the race of life, free society is such that he knows he can better his condition; he knows that there is no fixed condition of labor for his whole life."[27]

Perhaps the popular American belief in meritocracy explains why our sense of economic class has remained practically unchanged across the decades. In 1972, 48 percent of Americans called themselves "working class," while another 44 percent called themselves "middle class."[28] By 2002, despite a 15 percent increase in income inequality,[29] these percentages were still 46 percent and 46 percent, with just 8 percent considering themselves either "lower class" or "upper class."[30]

If you are a French intellectual you might say that this is evidence of some sort of "false consciousness" among the proletariat. But most people believe that America offers a decent chance to prosper, however they choose to define prosperity.

Politicians have denied this core American truth at their peril, occasionally leading to comical moments in American politics. Back in 1972, Democratic presidential candidate George McGovern delivered a campaign speech to blue-collar workers at a rubber factory near Akron, Ohio. He announced his plan, if elected, to raise estate taxes and reduce inheritances dramatically—and redistribute the money to people like those assembled. He felt sure his message of redistributive fairness would strike a chord with his working-class audience. To McGovern's shock, he was booed.

We might make the (correct) observation that an inheritance is inconsistent with an heir's earned success, and there is no evidence that inherited wealth brings any happiness to people who inherit. But people aspire to rise enough to leave something to their kids or to charity. That is why polls find Americans believe the estate tax is the most unfair tax in the entire system.[31] It offends their sense of meritocratic fairness, not due to any merit on the part of heirs, but because people who honestly earn their money should not have it confiscated and redistributed, even after death.

MAYBE YOU'RE THINKING at this point that, of course, opportunity is real in America. But it's not the *only* thing. Some people are lucky, some people are born rich, and some people have access to better schools and colleges than other people. Other people are born poor, suffer from discrimination or handicaps, or live in areas where good schools are few. I was born into a family without much money but was lucky to have excellent parents who valued honesty, thrift, and education. I learned from an early age that hard work and self-discipline led to things I wanted. Other people aren't so lucky in their upbringing.

Good parents are only one kind of good luck. Studies show that good-looking people find it easier to get ahead in life. Throughout their careers, taller men have higher earnings than shorter men, and thin women with more attractive faces have the highest socioeconomic status all through life.[32] (I'm not sure you need a study to figure this out, but there you are.)

If equality of opportunity is not universal, should we throw out the whole idea of meritocratic fairness? Of course not. First, you're living in a dream world (or you have tenure) if you really believe merit doesn't matter. Everyone can think of times when things went well as a direct, observable result of hard work. Thinking a little harder, people can also come up with cases in which they were punished at work or in life for laziness, incompetence, free riding, or plain stupidity. I can think of lots of such cases in my own life.

Second, we have to build our system based on our values and aspirations. Even if success sometimes comes down to connections and good luck, it would be a mistake to build our system on the idea that this is all that matters. Even if only half of the outcomes in life were due to merit—a dubious assertion—we need to gear our system to the part under our control. Otherwise, we have no incentive to be industrious, honest, innovative, and optimistic. Do we really want to teach our kids that if they're not pretty and thin, they probably won't get very far in life? Do we want to teach them that it's alright to take things from others?

Third, and most importantly, if we reject the ideals of opportunity and meritocratic fairness, we will get a system in which outcomes really are just based on luck or political power. In a 2005 study of twenty-nine countries, researchers at Harvard and the Massachusetts Institute of Technology found that where taxes are higher and money is redistributed through social programs, citizens are much more likely to believe that luck, not merit, is the driving force behind success.[33] So, in countries like Italy, Spain, and Uruguay, at least half the population believes luck determines incomes and about twice as much of GDP is redistributed in social spending as in the United States.

The link between redistribution and citizens' cynicism isn't just a coincidence. The same study showed that economic outcomes in countries like Italy and Spain are disconnected from merit and hard work precisely *because* citizens demand government social programs and wealth redistribution. If people believe that economic outcomes are a product of luck, birth, connections, or corruption, they demand more and more forced wealth redistribution. This rewards political power and connections, as citizens, corporations, and interest groups lobby for favors, not excellence in the marketplace.

Simply put, if people believe they are rewarded for their merit, they'll get a system in which that's true. If they think it's all rigged or based on luck, then the system will end up that way.

Some politicians say that, for the sake of fairness, the U.S. needs to raise taxes on the entrepreneurial class—to make the "millionaires and billionaires," pay their "fair share." Unknowingly, these leaders are weakening America. They are damaging the possibility of achieving the kind of opportunity society they believe does not exist and moving the nation further and further away from the vision of the Founders.

If the opportunity society is becoming a myth, it is not because of income inequality. It is because of the leaders who insist that opportunity is not real and encourage policies that redistribute more and more income. They are moving America from a culture of aspiration to a culture of envy.

SOME OF MY progressive friends argue that my characterization of redistributive fairness is, well, not fair. Sure, progressives want more equality, they say, but all that really means is that they want to bring the bottom *up*, not bring the top *down* or equalize everybody. I don't buy this argument because I don't think it stands up to scrutiny. You simply can't get much more income equality without bringing the top down.

To many, it is an article of faith that income inequality in America is exploding, and the rich are getting richer while everyone else is stagnating or getting poorer. This seems certain to be one of the central arguments of the political left in the coming years. Yet a great deal of economic analysis today questions these "facts."

First, income inequality measures almost always neglect to consider things like changes in household size, the prices of goods and services people consume, and the value of services from the government. As a result, Northwestern University economist Robert Gordon states that the rise of inequality in America has been "exaggerated in both magnitude and timing."[34]

Second, the increases in inequality are not because the poor and middle class are worse off than in the past, according to Cornell University economist Richard Burkhauser. Inequality increases are mostly due to the fact that the top 1 percent of earners have gotten a lot more prosperous over the years.[35] Using data from the government's Current Population Survey, Burkhauser looks at the bottom 99 percent of earners to measure inequality growth in this group and finds almost none. Furthermore, the bottom 99 percent have not stagnated. According to the Congressional Budget Office, every income quintile has seen a real increase in purchasing power of at least 18 percent over the past thirty years.[36]

So, there have been substantial income increases at the very top of the pyramid—the "1 percent" in the rhetoric of the Occupy Wall Street movement. But that growth hasn't occurred at the *expense* of the 99 percent. Increasing income equality as a social goal means either you don't understand the evidence, or you think it is desirable per se to punish people at the top *because they are rich*. There's no way around this fact.

This logic relies on a kind of zero-sum reasoning: that the rich are rich only because the rest of us are not and that the wealthy can only get better off if the rest of us get worse off. Such a world-view has been debunked by two hundred years of economic data. Virtually every economist since Adam Smith has demonstrated that productive activity grows the size of the pie. Entrepreneurs create new economic activity, which creates jobs, opportunity, and economic growth. A farm or a factory can create value and wealth for both owners and workers via products that come into existence through their combined effort. Obviously management can abuse labor (and vice versa). But were it not for capitalists, workers would have no jobs at all.

THE REDISTRIBUTIONIST GOAL is not really one of bringing up the bottom, then. Effectively, it is to achieve economic *sameness*. The famous economist Arthur Okun, chairman of President Lyndon Johnson's Council of Economic Advisers and one of the most influential economists in the past one hundred years, put it this way:

> . . . incomes that match productivity have no ethical appeal. Equality in the distribution of incomes . . . as well as in the distribution of rights would be my *ethical* preference. Abstracting from the costs and the consequences, I would prefer more equality of income to less and would like complete equality best of all. . . . To extend the domain of rights and give every citizen an equal share of the national income would give added recognition to the moral worth of every citizen.[37]

This brings us to the most unfair aspect of this kind of anti-meritocratic thinking: To get to the ideal of sameness, somebody has to decide what and how much to take from whom and how to redistribute it. Who does that? You know the answer: The government does. The government decides how much of people's money to take and in what form—income, investments, savings, transactions, or whatever. It decides whether to give it to others in a welfare check or farm subsidy, or whether to give them services like medical care.

Everyone knows that America needs a functioning government and critical public services. I am happy to help pay for the fire department that puts out the fire in your house (and mine). The problem arises when the government takes from you and gives something to me, *not* to provide critical services, but just to make us more equal for reasons of redistributive "fairness."

I reject any argument that bureaucrats are fairer than markets. There is nothing fair about corporate welfare and bailouts, or pork-barrel government spending. Fairness has nothing to do with the billions of dollars to save General Motors and Chrysler from bankruptcy. It has nothing to do with the stimulus spending of the past three years.

Finally, there is something radically depressing about the logic of redistributive fairness. Those who believe in it assume that simply by writing a check to increase someone's buying power, the recipient will have a more fulfilling life. Notice that its proponents speak only rarely about inequality in the things that matter most to people, the institutions of meaning in life, like faith, charity, and happiness. They speak about the money.

A MORAL SYSTEM requires fairness. A fair system in an opportunity society rewards merit. In contrast, an *un*fair system redistributes resources simply to derive greater income equality. That is a world in which, in the words of Rudyard Kipling, "all men are paid for existing and no man must pay for his sins."[38]

America does not have a perfect opportunity society. But if we want to move closer to that ideal, we must define fairness as meritocracy, embrace an economic system that rewards merit, and work tirelessly for more equal opportunity for all, rich and poor alike.

The system that makes all this possible, of course, is free enterprise. When I work harder or longer hours in the free enterprise system, I am generally paid more than if I work less in the same job. Investments in my education translate into market rewards. Clever ideas usually garner more rewards than bad ones, as judged not by a politburo, but rather by large groups of citizens in the marketplace. True fairness makes free enterprise not just an economic alternative. It makes it a moral imperative.

I want to emphasize two things that I am *not* arguing.

First, I am not arguing for anything like corporate cronyism. I believe in the free enterprise system; I do not believe in the unjust allocation of rewards to anyone, rich or poor. I am wholly opposed to the corporate bailouts in 2008 and 2009, just as I am opposed to government subsidies for energy companies and tax loopholes to favored industries. Corporate cronyism, like statism, is just another way to wreck competition and freedom. Further, lurking behind almost every case of uncompetitive business practices are perpetrators who have a close relationship with government power.

Second, I am not arguing that there is no role for government in this system. Private markets can and do fail, and the state may have a responsibility to act in some of these cases. Most serious economists also believe that a social safety net in a civilized country is appropriate to prevent the worst predations of poverty. When the government focuses on these things, it assists the free enterprise system. But when the government bails out companies suffering from poor business practices or redistributes goods, services, and income simply for the sake of "fairness," it lowers opportunity and impoverishes people in many ways.

Still, you might be asking, "What about the poor?" Distributing income according to merit might be good and just, but we all recognize that some people won't be able to take care of themselves properly. Fair or not, we want to help with more than just a minimum government safety net.

This brings us to the third moral promise of the free enterprise system and arguably its greatest achievement, helping the poor all around the world.

# 4

## A SYSTEM FOR GOOD SAMARITANS

One of the most famous parables in the Christian Bible is the story of the Good Samaritan.[1]

Jesus was asked by a follower, "Who is my neighbor?" In response, Jesus told the story of a Jew traveling along the road from Jerusalem to Jericho. The man was attacked by thieves, who robbed him and left him stripped and beaten. As he lay there half dead, two Jewish religious leaders—a priest and a Levite—found him on the road. Instead of helping the man, they passed on the other side. After them came a Samaritan, who, seeing the man, had compassion and stopped to help. Despite many years of hatred between Samaritans and Jews, the Samaritan bound up the injured man's wounds, fed him, clothed him, and took him to an inn. Before departing, the Good Samaritan left money and instructions for the innkeeper to ensure that the man was cared for.

The point of the parable is clear: People have a duty to help those in need—not only those close to them, but also strangers and even enemies. Preoccupation with our own affairs is no excuse for ignoring the vulnerable. No matter what your religious beliefs, you probably agree with this, which is why everyone—Christian, Muslim, Jew, atheist, whatever—knows what a "Good Samaritan" is and believes there should be more of them.

Today, many believe that political progressives are the Good Samaritans because they support government welfare programs that help the poor. During the heated federal budget battles of 2011, one liberal Christian group took out full-page ads in a national newspaper with the provocative question, "What Would Jesus Cut?"[2] The ad asked readers to sign a petition asking Congress to oppose any policies that involved cutting domestic and international programs that benefit the poor, especially children.

In this construction, of course, proponents of limited government and the free enterprise system are the priest and the Levite who just walk by as the poor and needy suffer. Capitalism creates incentives for people to be greedy and selfish, and to pursue their own economic interests regardless of the damage they cause. This may even be too charitable: Many argue that free marketeers are like the *robbers*. Free enterprise helps the rich get richer at the expense of the poor. Capitalism doesn't just allow people to ignore the injured man in the ditch; the system throws him in and then makes people ever more likely to be unmoved by his plight.

Supporters of the welfare state thus levy two related moral charges against free enterprise. The first is that it makes the rich richer and doesn't help the poor. The second is that it is morally corrupting; it makes people indifferent to the suffering of others.

The first charge is the easiest to debunk. While free enterprise may create significant income inequality, it actually helps *everyone*. True, the rich may get very rich in a free market economy, but the poor get much richer too. As Senator Marco Rubio of Florida has remarked, "the free enterprise system has lifted more people out of poverty than all the government anti-poverty programs combined."[3] The evidence shows that the senator is correct.

The second charge is more interesting. Certainly, the economic collapse has exposed plenty of villains—from bailed out Wall Street CEOs with gold-plated exit packages to criminals like Bernie Madoff—whom progressives love to point to as examples of the moral turpitude of unfettered capitalism. But those are just easy potshots—crooks and corporate cronies are not part of a healthy free enterprise system. I will show that America's everyday capitalists—the millions who work honestly and support free enterprise over government redistribution—are the real Good Samaritans in society.

FREE ENTERPRISE has made life better today than at any time in history.

Economic historians have established that in 1800, the average person had a standard of living no better than people living in the Stone Age.[4] Of course, some people were better off than others. A handful of the world's population in 1800 were rich (by the standards of the day) and lived in relative splendor, but the masses did not eat better, sleep more comfortably, clothe themselves more warmly, or shelter themselves from the elements more snugly than their ancestors did 100,000 years earlier.

Life in 1800 was incomparably worse than it is today in every physical way: shorter, more dangerous, and filled with sickness. In the mid-eighteenth century, even in the world's most advanced cities like London, only one-quarter of the population could expect to live beyond five years of age.[5]

For the lucky few who made it out of childhood in the eighteenth century, the life that awaited them was difficult and short. According to one historian of the period, "violence, disorder, and brutal punishment were a part of the normal background of life."[6] Disease was rampant and food was short. In the great cities of London and Paris, "plague, disease, or famine would strike every decade or so, killing as many as 10,000 people in a few weeks."[7]

Modern Americans tend to take for granted that our lives will become more prosperous as we age, and that our kids will enjoy even better lives than we do. And for good reason: The average American enjoys 35 percent more real income today than thirty years ago, and every income bracket has benefited.[8] Americans think that material progress is, if not the natural order of things, at least a natural right. But this faith in economic progress is a new phenomenon, historically. Before 1800, children could not expect a better life than their parents, grandparents, or any ancestors, for that matter. World GDP per capita actually fell slightly from AD 1 to AD 1000, and grew just 47 percent from 1000 to 1820.[9]

So for all of history until about 200 years ago, the world was desperately poor. But then something happened: the Industrial Revolution, and what economist Gregory Clark has termed the "Great Divergence." In one set of countries, average prosperity in the 19th century began to rocket upward. In these lucky countries, income, standard of living, health, literacy—in short, every measurable aspect of well-being—saw a dramatic increase, unparalleled in history. In the unlucky countries left behind by the Industrial Revolution—the rest of the world—incomes and quality of life stayed more or less where they had been for centuries.

America was one of the lucky countries. The explosion in better living standards can be illustrated with a handful of statistics.

In 1850, life expectancy at birth in the United States was 38.3.[10] By 2010, it was 78.[11] The literacy rate in the United States rose from 80 percent in 1870 to 99 percent today.[12] And real per capita GDP increased twenty-two-fold from 1820 to 1998.[13]

The primary beneficiaries of the Industrial Revolution were the poorest members of society, not the richest. It is easy to think of the misery portrayed in Charles Dickens' novels and imagine that the Industrial Revolution had made life worse for people who might have happily lived an agrarian life. In truth, after the early 1800s, living standards for the poorest Americans and Europeans began to rise to levels unimaginable a few years earlier. Until the Industrial Revolution, for example, formal education was reserved for the wealthy who could afford to pay and who could afford to keep their children out of the workforce. There was no education for the poor in America until the first public school opened in Boston in 1817. With the Industrial Revolution, public schools quickly spread to educate the masses. Within a century from the construction of the first public school, laws mandated primary education in most of the United States, and 72 percent of children had completed grade school.[14] To be sure, there was much progress still to be made, and during the Industrial Revolution, life for the working class was hard. But compared to what had come before, the Industrial Revolution's accompanying economic and social benefits were the greatest antipoverty program ever known.[15]

After more than a century, the Industrial Revolution's blessings ultimately began to spread beyond Europe and America. As the twentieth century progressed, the number of lucky countries around the world grew. As a result, global poverty is decreasing radically, with real world GDP per capita today many times larger than it was in 1820.

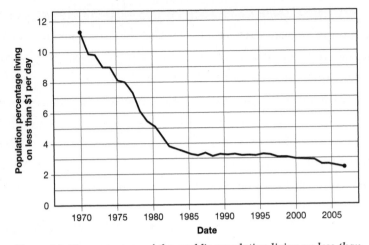

***Figure 4.1.*** *The percentage of the world's population living on less than $1 per day has fallen dramatically. (Source: Maxim Pinkovskiy and Xavier Sala-i-Martin, "Parametric Estimations of the world distribution of income," NBER Working Paper 15433, http://www.nber.org/papers /w15433.pdf.)*

The improvements have been massive even in recent decades. The number of people in the world living on a dollar a day—a traditional poverty measure—has fallen by 80 percent since 1970, from 11.2 percent of the world's population to 2.3 percent.[16]

How did the Industrial Revolution happen? How did the world become, if not rich, at least dramatically less poor than it had been two centuries earlier? The answer is free enterprise, or what philosopher Michael Novak calls "democratic capitalism."[17] During the last two hundred years, there has been an unprecedented emergence of free societies and markets, accumulation of capital, and expansion of trade. The sudden emergence of free enterprise unleashed human creativity and ingenuity and brought about a previously inconceivable surge in living standards. Free enterprise is the reason that in two centuries, the world has progressed from an almost universally impoverished one to a world that is not.

Of course, there is still great poverty around the world. And here's the reason: free enterprise still has not spread widely enough. If you look at where poverty is disappearing fastest in the world, you'll find capitalism on the rise. According to the World Bank, China alone has accounted for more than 75 percent of poverty reduction in the entire developing world over the past two decades. How? This occurred not through communism, but through China's economic gains since Mao's death and its entry into world markets. From 1990 to 2006, just sixteen years, the inflation-adjusted value of Chinese exports to the United States increased by more than 1,000 percent.[18] According to the World Bank, 400 million Chinese were lifted out of absolute poverty between 1981 and 2001.[19] China has a long way to go to become a truly free and prosperous country, but the gains it *has* made have come from its experiments with capitalism.

Where has free enterprise been most elusive? In sub-Saharan Africa, home to the world's most impoverished countries. Africa's poorest countries include Burundi and the Democratic Republic of the Congo.[20] In these countries, citizens live on less than $1 per day.[21] Neither of these countries has a functional free enterprise system. Trade is restricted, property rights are weak, and markets are subverted by the government. Economists have shown again and again that this lack of economic freedom keeps people in poverty.[22] People have difficulty establishing private ownership of property, and bureaucratic systems make starting enterprises difficult or impossible. Low borrowing and investment mean little or no accumulation of capital, weak business formation, low job creation, and virtually no economic progress.

That is the real reason that misery persists in Africa, despite at least $1 trillion in foreign aid over the last fifty years.[23] Foreign aid—even if it were administered in an efficient, noncorrupt way—

cannot lift up more than a small percentage of a country's poor. To raise up a whole nation, a system that creates wealth, like America's, is needed. That system is free enterprise.[24]

William Easterly, a professor of economics at New York University and one of the leading experts on international development, spent years researching how and why economies develop. He concluded that capitalism is the "good guy," not the "bad guy." He writes, "The number of poor people who can't afford food for their children is a lot smaller than it used to be–thanks to capitalism. Capitalism didn't create malnutrition, it reduced it." Easterly adds that "profit-motivated capitalism is still the best case for the poor."[25]

The most compelling evidence for free enterprise comes from comparing similar countries that took different paths. Consider the case of North Korea and South Korea. One country embraced capitalism, while the other rejected it. Both Koreas were poor, and had the same GDP per capita just sixty years ago. Many socialists in the West believed that the North's Stalinist system of central planning would prove more effective than the South's market-based approach.

We all know how things turned out on the Korean peninsula. Today, North Korea is horribly poor and its people are starving. It also has the distinction of being the least free country in the world.[26] Meanwhile, South Korea is both the thirty-seventh freest country in the world and the thirteenth richest.[27] South Korea's GDP per capita is sixteen times that of North Korea.[28]

Free enterprise means richer, healthier, and happier people worldwide. Each year, the "Economic Freedom Index" by The Fraser Institute (a Canadian think tank) ranks countries along forty-two dimensions, from personal choice in goods and services, to ease of voluntary exchange, to freedom to compete

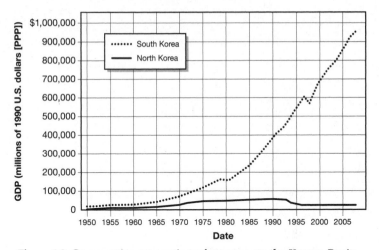

***Figure 4.2.*** *Comparative economic performance on the Korean Penin-sula. (Source: Angus Maddison, "Statistics on World Population, GDP and Per Capita GDP, 1-2008 AD." Groningen: The Groningen Growth and Development Centre. Available at http://www.ggdc.net /MADDISON/oriindex.htm.)*

economically, to the security of privately owned property.[29] The index measures a country's degree of free enterprise. It finds that average citizens in economically free countries are prosperous, by world standards. In countries that are not free, people are poor.

In the freest nations (the top fifth), the average annual income is eighteen times that in the least-free nations (the lowest fifth). The problem is not that there is unequal distribution of money in the world. The problem is that there is unequal distribution of free enterprise.

But freedom doesn't just correlate with income; freer people are healthier too. In the freest countries, people live about twenty years longer, on average, than people in the least free countries. There's no surprise here, of course. Richer countries have better health care than poorer countries. Nevertheless, it is still worth pointing out that free enterprise and prosperity have huge human consequences.

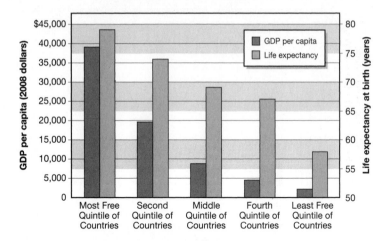

***Figure 4.3.*** *GDP per capita and life expectancy vary dramatically according to economic freedom between countries. (Source: James Gwartney, Joshua Hall, and Robert Lawson.* Economic Freedom of the World 2010 Annual Report. *Fraser Institute. http://www .fraserinstitute.org/uploadedFiles/fraser-ca/Content/research-news/ research/publications/economic-freedom-of-the-world-2010.pdf; GDP per capita and life expectancy data are from the World Bank* World Development Indicators. *http://data.worldbank.org/indicator [accessed 2011].)*

Skeptics say that all this tells us nothing about whether free enterprise helps poor people *within* countries. Maybe capitalism raises the income for the top 1 percent significantly, while leaving the poor in desperate straits. That would still make the "average" citizen look richer, but it would make no difference for the poor. For example, if you and I start out with salaries of $50,000 and then you double your salary to $100,000 and I don't, our average salary rises to $75,000, but I'm no better off than I was.

However, if we look at the numbers a little more closely, the true picture emerges. The data show that the poorest 10 percent of citizens in the freest twenty countries earn about six times more than the poorest 10 percent in the least-free countries.

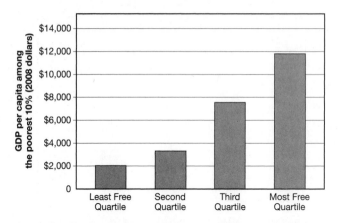

***Figure 4.4.*** *The poor are best off in economically free countries. (Source: James Gwartney, Joshua Hall, and Robert Lawson,* Economic Freedom of the World 2010 Annual Report. *Fraser Institute. http://www.fraserinstitute.org/uploadedFiles/fraser-ca /Content/research-news/research/publications/economic-freedom -of-the-world-2010.pdf.)*

These data show correlation, not causation, but there is no sleight of hand here. Many economists have proven that free enterprise *causes* prosperity by taking into account other explanations (like natural resources) and isolating the effects of free enterprise policies on economic growth. They have also indicated that growth follows freedom over time. And they have shown exactly how free enterprise rewards people for working hard and taking risks and, in turn, how this leads to wealth accumulation and prosperity for everyone.[30]

FREE ENTERPRISE creates growth and lifts up the rich and poor alike by giving entrepreneurs an incentive to create, earn their success, and keep the rewards. The prosperity passes to others because entrepreneurs generate jobs and growth, compete for workers, and raise wages. Alternatively, when regulations are too harsh, the police are too corrupt, and the taxes are too punitive, there is little incentive to innovate and create. Poor people stay poor.

Rather than looking at the massive gains that free enterprise has created for the poor, critics complain that capitalism allows some people to get much richer than others, leading to the kind of economic inequality here in the United States. They're right; economic inequality is higher in America than it is in a country like Cuba. But surely this argument can't stand against the free enterprise system. Would you rather live in a place where everyone is very poor (except, maybe, a handful of kleptocrats who run the government)? Or in a place where everyone has a fairly high, basic standard of living, a handful of people have a lot more than others, and if you work hard and get lucky, you can join them?

Moreover, measures of income inequality radically overstate the true difference between economic classes in free societies. In 2009, the top fifth of American households had an average pretax income of $170,844, while the bottom fifth had an average income of $11,552.[31] This is a significant difference: The average income of the top fifth is sixteen times the average income of the bottom fifth. But let's look at consumption, what people actually do with the money they have. When we look at the money people actually lived on in 2009, we see that the wealthiest fifth of Americans spent less than five times what the poorest fifth spent.[32]

Even more important than the equality in the amount of consumption is the equality in the *type* of consumption. One recent study of the American poor found that the average American household in poverty (as defined by the government) had air conditioning, cable television, multiple TVs, and, if they had male children, an Xbox or PlayStation video-game console.[33] These modern conveniences are unthinkable in other parts of the world, but they are commonplace in America, even among lower-income groups.

Consider also that virtually everybody in America has a car. A few people own $200,000 Porsches, and many people own $10,000 used Kias. One may be more fun to drive, but both will get people to work. The cars are *functionally* nearly the same. In America and many other prosperous, free countries, both the billionaire and the manual worker own their own cars and have the freedom to travel around. That is the true miracle, and free enterprise—not government edict—made it so. Or, as the late Andy Warhol commented back in 1975:

> What's great about this country is that America
> started the tradition where the richest consumers buy
> essentially the same things as the poorest. You can
> be watching TV and see Coca-Cola, and you know
> that the President drinks Coke, Liz Taylor drinks
> Coke, and just think, you can drink Coke, too.
> A Coke is a Coke and no amount of money can get
> you a better Coke than the one the bum on the cor-
> ner is drinking. All the Cokes are the same and all
> the Cokes are good. Liz Taylor knows it, the Presi-
> dent knows it, the bum knows it, and you know it.[34]

Here's the bottom line: Capitalism and free enterprise have lifted everyone up. It is truly galling to see the 2011 Occupy Wall Street protesters demonstrate with signs that read, "We are the 99%," as if they were somehow treated unfairly by any objective world standard. These protesters, as privileged Americans, are part of the world's *1 percent*.

Some people live in a materialistic world of "keeping up with the Joneses," and inequality is all they're worried about. In that case, then communism, authoritarianism, totalitarianism may be the best systems, because they keep almost everyone poor. But if quality of life matters to you, then you should support free enterprise unequivocally. It pulls millions of people out of poverty every year, increases their health and life expectancy, and gives them the possibility of something even greater.

In dealing with poverty here and around the world, welfare and foreign aid are a Band-Aid. Free enterprise is a cure.


FREE ENTERPRISE has eradicated poverty all over the world for billions of people. But does that mean that free enterprise is a moral system—or simply that it happens to have beneficial effects? On the surface, free enterprise can seem like a pretty passive kind of virtue: I pursue my own self-interest, this creates value, and other people—especially poor people—reap the rewards of a more prosperous society. Is it possible that ethically neutral—or even selfish—behavior just happens to have happy side-effects in the case of free enterprise? Lots of people—even some who call themselves libertarians and conservatives—think that for society to get richer, it automatically must adopt Gordon Gekko's famous creed in the movie *Wall Street*: "Greed is good."

The second charge that opponents of free enterprise levy against it is that it rewards rotten people. The more I work for myself, the argument goes, the more the free enterprise system enriches me personally. If I take time out to actively help others,

I sacrifice time that I could have spent further enriching myself (economists call this an *opportunity cost*). Therefore, the more I can keep the rewards of my own productivity, the less charitable I will tend to be. So, opponents say, capitalism naturally makes people rapacious.

A counterargument is that free enterprise actually makes people *more* virtuous. The line of reasoning here is more complex and requires a bit more concentration, but, in summary, is this: The free enterprise system requires a culture of optimism and trust to function correctly—a positive-sum, win-win mentality, and a desire for everyone to be better off. For many people, it produces more prosperity than they need to meet their daily requirements, a surplus that many will choose to direct to charitable purposes.[35] Moreover, people who believe in free enterprise reject the idea that the government is responsible for solving all social problems. For this reason, people who believe in the free enterprise system are more likely than others to take responsibility for the neediest members of their communities.

So does free enterprise make people self-absorbed and morally corrupt? Or does it make people better, more socially responsible human beings? The data show unequivocally that the latter answer is correct.

THE UNITED STATES is a very generous country. Seventy to eighty percent of American households donate money every year; the average household contributes more than $1,000 annually. About one-third of these charitable gifts go to religious causes to support churches, synagogues, and so on. The rest goes to secular activities, such as education, health, and social welfare. Also, money isn't all that Americans give: Between 50 and 60 percent of Americans formally volunteer their time each year, giving an average of almost fifty hours.[36]

Charitable donations in America add up to approximately $300 billion annually. That's more than the entire GDP of countries like Finland, Portugal, and Peru.[37] About three-quarters comes from private individuals, with the rest from corporations and foundations. No developed country approaches Americans' level of giving and volunteering. In 1995, Americans, gave three and a half times as much to causes and charities per capita as the French, seven times as much as the Germans, and fourteen times as much as the Italians. In 1998, Americans were 15 percentage points more likely to volunteer than the Dutch, 21 points more likely than the Swiss, and 32 points more likely than the Germans. These differences are not attributable to demographic characteristics such education, income, age, sex, or marital status.[38]

Americans are not charitable just because they're rich. True, the rich do give the most money. But remarkably, the working poor give a higher percentage of their income to charity than the wealthy and much more than the middle class.[39] Charitable giving appears to be part of most Americans' DNA; it is not just the *noblesse oblige* of the wealthy few.

But perhaps the most remarkable fact about charity in America is how highly it correlates with ideology and beliefs about the role of government. People who believe in the free enterprise system simply give a lot more—both time and money—than people who don't. In a nutshell, people who believe in limited government privately give much more than their statist neighbors.

Consider attitudes about income inequality. In 1996, people who disagreed that "the government has a responsibility to reduce income inequality" gave, on average, four times as much money to charity each year as people who agreed that the government

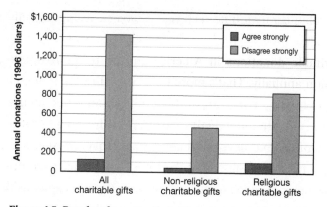

**Figure 4.5.** *People who agree that, "the government has a responsibility to reduce income inequality," give far less privately to charity than those who disagree. (Source: 1996 General Social Survey. National Opinion Research Center, University of Chicago.)*

should equalize incomes more. People who disagreed *strongly* with greater forced redistribution gave eleven times more, on average, than those who agreed strongly.[40]

This pattern of giving holds for nonmonetary charity as well. For example, in 1996, Americans who believed that the government has a responsibility to reduce income inequality were substantially less likely to volunteer their time than people who did not believe this. People who stated in 2002 that they thought the government was "spending too little money on welfare" were less likely than those saying the government is "spending too much money on welfare" to donate blood, give directions to someone on the street, or return extra change to a cashier. Ironically, they were less likely even to offer food or money to a homeless person.[41]

People who believe in redistribution are more likely to treat someone uncharitably in subtle ways. For example, they will be late for professional appointments. In one fascinating experiment, a team of researchers from Estonia, Morocco, and the United

States interviewed students in those three countries about their views on punctuality. They found that, regardless of the cultures in the study, people with collectivist views also have a more liberal view of what is acceptably late to arrive for a meeting.[42]

What explains these patterns? Redistributionists generally believe meaningful social action resides principally with the government. Individuals shouldn't have to give their money or time to help the less fortunate. That's the job of the state. Ralph Nader commented, "A society that has more justice is a society that needs less charity."[43] Instead of giving to charity, redistributionists vote for progressive policies and candidates who will increase the responsibilities of the government.

Is voting just a different way of giving to help others? Not quite. Voting for a candidate doesn't mean you are going to pay any more in taxes than your capitalist neighbor who votes differently than you do. It might make you feel unselfish—hey, I'm willing to raise my own taxes!—but it's only an expression of your views, not an actual sacrifice unless yours is the swing vote in a fifty-fifty election. Good intentions are not gifts, and by themselves, they don't help the poor.

In November 2011, a reporter from the *Daily Caller* revealed the redistributionist attitude in a series of interviews with progressive millionaires protesting on Capitol Hill in favor of higher tax rates for the wealthy. She offered each the opportunity to make a voluntary contribution to the U.S. Treasury through the website Pay.gov. None of the wealthy Americans were willing to donate a cent.[44]

While progressive politicians and the occupiers of Wall Street hurl invective at capitalists for their selfishness, the evidence proves that they're wrong. On average, people who support free enterprise over growing government are vastly more privately generous than those who oppose it. They understand that the government can't fix all or even most ills, and that individuals and communities share the responsibility to take care of society's weakest members.

A CURIOUS FACT about the link between charity and free enterprise is that giving rewards the giver. It really *is* better to give than to receive.

Prosperity and charity are strongly and positively related. It makes sense that higher income leads to more giving. But new research shows that giving actually stimulates personal prosperity. Analysis controlling for education, age, race, and all the other outside explanations for increases in giving and income revealed that a dollar donated to charity leads to approximately $3.75 in extra income to the giver.[45]

How can this be? The research suggests that private giving transforms people, even physiologically. It lowers their stress levels, for example. In one experiment, senior citizens were asked to give massages to babies, the idea being that they would do this nice thing with no expectation of a return. Afterward, the adults were found to have markedly lower stress hormone levels in their brains than beforehand.[46] The implication is that if you are stressed, you should do something charitable for someone else.

Givers are more popular and more admired than nongivers, which should directly affect their prosperity. In one British university study, participants were given a sum of money and asked in front of others to choose whether to keep it for themselves or give it to a public fund.[47] They were also told that everything in the public fund would be totaled, the amount of money doubled, and then the money would be divided equally among the participants.

In other words, *everyone* would benefit from an individual's public spiritedness, even the selfish people who decided to simply pocket their own cash.

The interesting part of the experiment came after the decisions were made about how to allocate the money. The participants then broke into small groups to choose a leader from among themselves. They did not know each other; all they knew was how the other participants had behaved during the giving experiment. In more than 80 percent of the cases, the groups selected as leader the individual who had placed the highest amount of money in the public fund. People see giving as a leadership quality.

These studies and many others suggest that giving can make people better off—even monetarily. What is true for individuals is also true for the country as a whole: Charity in America stimulates American economic growth. Per capita charity and per capita GDP in the United States have moved in tandem over the years, with the former increasing by 190 percent in real terms since 1954 and the latter by 150 percent. Evidence that the two forces stimulate each other comes from analysis of how past values of one variable affect future values of the other. This analysis shows that a 10 percent increase in charity per person provokes a 3 percent increase in GDP.

Put in dollar terms, $1 of private charity can increase GDP by about $19, an excellent rate of return (especially in these tough economic times).[48] Indeed, charity is a much better kind of "stimulus" than government spending. Even the most liberal economists estimate a return to government spending of around $1.50 for every $1 spent, and many find it is actually less than a dollar.[49]

Givers get rewards that are more important than money, too. For example, the data show that givers are happier and healthier than nongivers. Americans who give charitably are 43 percent more likely to say they are very happy than people who don't, according to one 2000 national survey. It doesn't matter whether people give to a church or a symphony orchestra: Religious and secular giving both leave people equally happy, and far happier than those who don't give. (And the more people give, the happier they get.)[50]

Do you want to improve a young person's life? Don't tell her to march with a sign demanding her rights to someone else's money. Teach her to give to others and volunteer. In one study, researchers followed a thousand teenagers over five years and measured the extent of their charitable attitudes and behaviors through such questions as, "For the job you expect to have in the future, how important is helping people?" and, "How often do you spend time performing community service outside school?" The teenagers who were the most giving were the least likely to be involved in street violence and teen pregnancies. They were also the least likely to experience stress and negative feelings.[51]

Charity exists in a kind of virtuous circle: people give their time and money because they recognize need and want to make life better for others. But in so doing, they also become better, more prosperous people. This in turn adds to economic growth and opportunity for the whole nation. For this reason, it is essential that the state not intervene in ways that will prevent people from acting charitably.

Unfortunately, the government thwarts private charity all the time. Consider this example. In 2006, Fairfax County, Virginia, adopted a policy (later reversed) to "help" the homeless. In order to prevent food poisoning, the county barred residents from giving food to the hungry on the street unless it was prepared in a county-approved kitchen. This policy disqualified the food produced by approximately half the operating shelters and churches that had previously fed the hungry, despite the fact that food poisoning from donated food had never been reported. It also made it illegal for someone to share a homemade sandwich with a homeless person. The results were, of course, entirely negative for the homeless, who were now more likely than before to eat genuinely dangerous food out of dumpsters. It also deprived a community of the opportunity to volunteer by working in a soup kitchen or simply by buying a homeless man a sandwich. These kinds of government interventions are thus doubly destructive; they hurt the people who they're meant to help and deny the helpers the opportunity to develop their moral lives and flourish through giving.[52]

WE DON'T HAVE TO ACCEPT the claims about free enterprise and its effects on the poor as a matter of faith. There is ample evidence about how the underprivileged are affected by capitalism and market economies. Free enterprise creates enormous opportunity and prosperity, including, especially, for the least among us.

Free enterprise advocates need to master the facts on this subject. Only then can they combat the common redistributionist argument that capitalism is good for the rich but not the poor, and that it corrupts us morally. The hard evidence clearly shows that free enterprise is the best system for lifting up the poorest in society and the best system for encouraging moral action on the part of private individuals.

Statism halts free enterprise's virtuous circle in its tracks. When we take away people's ability to prosper privately, they work less, earn less, spend less, and create fewer jobs for others. When the government crowds out private charity, people give less and we all rely even more on the government.

This destructive dynamic hurts everyone in the income distribution. Frankly, I am not very concerned about the rich: They will do just fine. I am concerned about the poor, who truly suffer when entrepreneurship and private charity are suffocated.

None of this is purely theoretical. For years, I have watched social democratic policies ravage the economy of my wife's home country, Spain. Government has grown, debt has grown, charity has withered in favor of government welfare, and private entrepreneurs have been vilified and harassed—all for the sake of the working man. The result is that today, unemployment in Spain stands at 21.2 percent, and at 46.2 percent for youths between ages sixteen and twenty-four.[53] The poor are the ones suffering most from thirty years of reliance on the bloated, inefficient Spanish government.

I am not arguing that the government has no role in helping the underprivileged. It does. Markets do not always function properly and a social safety net does have a place in American society. In the second part of this book, I offer more specific information about what the government can and should do to help the poor in a free enterprise system.

But the moral of this chapter, I hope, is clear. If you love the poor, then you should privately give more and fight for free enterprise for everyone. It's what the Good Samaritan would do.

# II

## Applying the Moral Case
## for Free Enterprise

# 5

## FACING THE FACTS ABOUT AMERICA'S *STATIST QUO*

An economist is out for a drive on a country road. Unfamiliar with anything outside the big city, he soon gets hopelessly lost. Spotting a lone farmhouse, he pulls over, knocks on the door, and asks the farmer for help. The farmer gives the economist careful directions back to the city.

The economist thanks the farmer and while turning to leave, he notices the house is flanked by a large field full of sheep. Always on the lookout for a profit-making opportunity, the economist poses this wager to the farmer: "I see you have a lot of sheep there, sir. If I can tell you the exact number in ten seconds, will you give me one of them?"

The farmer, amused by the wager, says, "There's no way you can tell how many sheep I have without counting them. You're on."

The economist immediately employs a complex set of analytic heuristic devices, refining his estimates in rapid succession until he reaches his conclusion: "You, sir, have 863 sheep."

"Why, that is just amazing," says the farmer. "That is exactly right!"

Being a man of his word, the farmer invites the economist to pick out any sheep he wants. The economist does so and walks back to his car with the animal in his arms. But before he departs, the farmer stops him.

"You know, I have a wager of my own. If I can tell you your profession, can I have my sheep back?"

The economist, amused, responds, "There's no way you could know my profession, given that we've only just met. You're on."

The farmer says, "You, sir, are an economist."

"Why, that is just amazing," says the economist. "How on earth did you know that?"

"Simple," says the farmer. "You got all the numbers right, but you're walking off with my dog."

I LIKE THIS STORY because I think it sums up the problems free enterprise advocates have today. They get the numbers right but get the most important things wrong. They're great at finding evidence that capitalism brings economic growth, but not as good translating that evidence into the real world and convincing people that free enterprise is the best system not only for prosperity, but also for a flourishing America.

The first four chapters of this book consisted of my best attempt to solve this problem—to make the moral case for free enterprise. In the next three chapters, I'll apply the lessons from those chapters to the issues the United States faces today, by doing three things.

First, I'll speak openly about what has gone wrong with the U.S. system. There has been a *bipartisan* slide toward big government over the last few decades, under both Democratic and Republican administrations. People must get over the idea that one election or one particular party will solve the problem—both parties have colluded in the vast expansion of the government over the last hundred years.

To be blunter, there is no guarantee that a Republican administration per se will bolster the culture and policies of free enterprise. In the worst case, Republican political victories can even set back the free enterprise cause, because Americans tend to become complacent when they don't see that the system is under clear assault. The bipartisan forces of big government creep back in, and the process of state expansion continues.

Second, I'll lay out what I believe the government should look like. It is insufficient to argue simply that the government is "too big." Free enterprise advocates have to be more specific and constructive than that, to rebuff the progressives' suspicions that all free marketeers *really* want is to help rich people (or that we are secretly storing up canned goods and waiting for the apocalypse).

Third, I'll offer tangible proposals for policy, not abstractions. Free enterprise's champions need to form an organized argument about economic growth, jobs, deficits, taxes, and the other key issues of our time—an argument that starts with the rock-solid moral case; uses facts and data to show that reform is necessary and urgent, provides principles for reform, and offers actual, specific policies.

AMERICANS ARE ambivalent when it comes to the role of the state. They say they love free enterprise and dislike big government, but over the last century they've let the public sector crowd out entrepreneurship and make deeper and deeper incursions into their lives.

As I noted at the beginning of this book, Americans say they consider free enterprise central to U.S. culture and success. A 2010 Gallup poll, for instance, showed that 86 percent of Americans had a positive image of free enterprise, while only 10 percent had a negative image.[1] According to a 2011 Gallup poll, 60 percent of Americans "strongly agreed" that "entrepreneurs are job creators."[2] (Incidentally, the same poll found that just 30 percent of Europeans felt the same way about entrepreneurs.)

By commanding majorities, Americans say they prefer limited government over an expansive welfare state. In early 2010, a *Washington Post*–ABC News poll asked Americans, "Generally speaking, would you say you favor smaller government with fewer services, or larger government with more services?" To this question, 38 percent favored the latter, while 58 percent preferred the former.[3]

Average Americans viscerally dislike big government. Most of their ordinary contacts with the government are pretty unpleasant. Remember how much fun it was the last time you had to go to the DMV? Have you ever tried calling the IRS's helpline for assistance filling out your tax returns?

So Americans profess a love for free enterprise and dislike "big government." But here's the paradox: They are more than willing to accept policies that do violence to the system they say they love. For example, a February 2011 NBC News/*Wall Street Journal* poll asked a thousand Americans whether it was acceptable to cut Social Security as a way to reduce the deficit. To this question, 77 percent of respondents said that it was either mostly unacceptable or totally unacceptable.[4] About half of Americans tell pollsters they are pretty comfortable with the idea that the U.S. should "redistribute wealth by heavy taxes on the rich."[5]

One explanation for this paradox is that Americans don't *really* love free enterprise as they say they do. They talk about it sentimentally. After all, *everything* was better in the old days. But in practice, Americans prefer a modern welfare state. This is the explanation I often hear from my progressive friends.

I don't think that's the real reason. I believe that most Americans still love and want the kind of freedom that the Founders envisioned. But a drift toward statism has happened so gradually that most haven't noticed it. It has happened because most people aren't really paying attention to the net growth of government. Americans are busy people, living private lives full of everyday jobs, church socials, and soccer practices. As the leader of a think tank dedicated to public policy, I would love it if Americans were as obsessed with policy as I am. But let's be realistic: most people don't have time to contemplate the potential damage each government bill—each tiny encroachment on their freedom—could cause.

Politicians have offered one policy compromise after another, from a government subsidy here to a hidden tax there. Slowly, people have become anaesthetized to the cumulative result. Over the years and decades, these gradual encroachments have re-oriented the U.S. toward European-style social democracy. Americans know something is wrong—which is why 81 percent say they are dissatisfied with the way the nation is being governed.[6] But they rarely make the connection between their free enterprise values and the statism they are getting instead.

WHEN AND HOW did this slide begin? The answer to this question depends upon whom you ask. Some say it started in 1912, with the election of Woodrow Wilson. Others say it began with Franklin D. Roosevelt's New Deal in the 1930s. Others say it started with Lyndon B. Johnson's Great Society programs of the 1960s.

Woodrow Wilson had a statist philosophy that today sounds quite academic; indeed, he held a PhD in political science and taught at Princeton years before his tenure in the White House. In 1887 he published the essay "Socialism and Democracy," in which he stated, "Men as communities are supreme over men as individuals. Limits of wisdom and convenience to the public control there may be: limits of principle there are, upon strict analysis, none."[7] Clearing away the rhetorical clutter in the last sentence, Wilson was asserting that there was *no* moral claim for limited government. This is why he believed there was no inherent moral difference between democracy and socialism—and what led to his belief in bureaucracy as a science.[8]

After he was elected president, Wilson sought to change the relationship of Americans to their government. His expansion of the state was massive. He created the Federal Reserve and agencies such as the Federal Trade Commission, increasing the size of government by almost 171 percent from 1913 to 1921, even after the buildup for World War I had ended and the war expenses had ceased.[9]

Wilson's efforts to increase the size and scope of government were carried forward a few decades later by Franklin D. Roosevelt. FDR met the Great Depression with government growth—"stimulus," in today's parlance. He created dozens of government agencies, from the Federal Housing Administration to the National Labor Relations Board, increasing the size of the federal government by 90 percent in the first eight years of his presidency (prior to America's entry into World War II).[10]

You probably learned in school that New Deal government programs were terrific for the American economy: They ended the worst period of unemployment in American history. But, what you learned is not true. Roosevelt's policies were *not* good for the economy. A 1935 study by the Brookings Institution, for example, examined the accomplishments of Roosevelt's National Recovery Administration (NRA), which regulated working conditions. According to the Brookings study, the NRA "on the whole retarded recovery."[11] In her bestselling book *The Forgotten Man*, economic historian Amity Shlaes shows that Roosevelt's spending heaped massive burdens on the country that more than offset the benefits of New Deal programs.[12] Shlaes argues that federal intervention helped prolong the Great Depression and made it deeper than it would otherwise have been. But government works like a ratchet, and government activity levels effectively never fell from their New Deal highs.

Lyndon B. Johnson picked up where FDR had left off in making the government central in the lives of millions of Americans. In his five years in office, Johnson increased the size of the federal government by 30 percent, but much more importantly, started a tidal wave of entitlements that inflated the size of government for many years after he left office. Johnson's legacy accomplishment was a set of programs collectively known as the Great Society, which dealt with education, medical care, urban problems, and transportation. The most ambitious part of it was known as the War on Poverty, which started programs from Head Start to food stamps.

Critics say generations of Americans were alienated from the workforce as a result of Johnson's programs, whole classes defined themselves as claimants on the U.S. government, and millions were consigned to squalid government housing and dignity-stripping welfare programs. As Ronald Reagan later quipped, "My friends, some years ago, the Federal Government declared war on poverty, and poverty won."[13] But at the time, the benefits of the programs seemed plausible to millions of Americans. Some of the most damaging welfare programs (such as Aid to Families with Dependent Children, or AFDC) have been reformed or replaced, but other Great

Society entitlements such as Medicare and Medicaid have yet to be reformed, and today threaten the viability of the U.S. economy.

These eras of Wilson, Roosevelt, and Johnson were profligate indeed, as the data in the next section will show. But there is a broader point to absorb: No particular president (except perhaps Calvin Coolidge) since the beginning of the twentieth century is really blameless when it comes to the explosion in government activity. Some like Wilson, Roosevelt, and Johnson were especially enthusiastic proponents of government growth, and some like Ronald Reagan held the line a little more than others. But none reversed the trends. In general, the twentieth century was the bipartisan century of big government.

SOCIAL DEMOCRACIES have been the norm in Western Europe since World War II. These systems are mildly utopian—based on a philosophy that the government can improve its citizens. But fundamentally, these systems are practical. They are motivated by a popular will to achieve higher levels of comfort, and lower levels of personal risk. Social democracies dominate in low-fertility, aging societies that are less comfortable with risk than they once might have been.

While professing some reliance on market forces, social democracies always build a large welfare state. Citizens enjoy early retirement ages, short working hours, generous unemployment benefits, and various types of socialized medicine. In social democracies, taxes tend to be high to pay for the large state and are extremely progressive to lower economic inequality. Regulation is generally complex and onerous, to achieve social goals and curb excess profitmaking.

With some exceptions like Germany, social democracies spend more money than their tax revenues can generate, so a large and increasing national debt is the norm. Economic growth is relatively low as the tax and regulatory systems leave entrepreneurs little incentive to innovate and work hard. In the long run, social democracies can produce dysfunctional governments and unstable economic and social situations like those in Spain, Greece, Portugal, and Italy—all of which are now being crushed under a burden of debt after years of profligate government spending but modest national output.

But America is different, right? Actually, no. Despite all the claims that America is organized on free market principles, over the decades it has become arguably just as socially democratic as Europe. Consider the following five facts.

### FACT #1. U.S. GOVERNMENT SPENDING HAS MASSIVELY EXPANDED AS A PERCENTAGE OF GDP.

In 1913, after passage of the Sixteenth Amendment that created the federal income tax, total government spending at all levels was about 8 percent of GDP. By 2010 it had risen to 36 percent, and by 2038 it will be 50 percent.[14]

Figure 5.1 is a graphic story of America's economic transformation. Ignore the World War I and World War II spending surges, and note only the broader trends. Big spending run-ups during the century never reverse, except for a brief period in the 1990s when the United States was disinvesting in its military. The increases are largely explained by massive entitlements, which politicians on both sides of the aisle have never meaningfully reined in.

The political right can crow all it wants about how America is a "conservative country," unlike, say, Spain—a country governed by the Spanish Socialist Workers Party for most of the past thirty years. But, according to OECD data, U.S. government spending relative to its GDP is approximately equal to Spain's.[15]

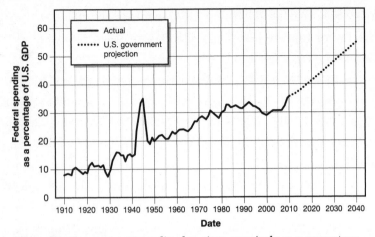

**Figure 5.1.** *Government spending has risen massively as a percentage of American GDP. (Source: Author's calculations.*[16])

FACT #2. AMERICA'S TAX SYSTEM IS HIGHLY PROGRESSIVE, WITH MORE AND MORE PEOPLE PAYING NO INCOME TAX AT ALL.

Progressive taxation means that the more you earn, the higher *percentage* you pay in taxes. For example, if you earn $34,500 today, your federal income tax rate on the last dollar you earn is 15 percent. If you earn $380,000, your rate is 35 percent. Most Americans do not object very much to this basic system. According to a November 2011 NBC News/*Wall Street Journal* poll, 56 percent of Americans prefer a graduated income tax system, while 40 percent of people prefer a system in which everyone pays the same rate.[17] Even conservative "flat tax" proposals almost always stipulate that low earners pay less—or even zero taxes.

Cutting the bottom out of the tax distribution has been a pronounced trend since the early 1990s, and it has silently exploded the progressivity of the American income tax system. While progressives have screamed that upper tax rates have not gotten more progressive year after year—they have gone up and down over the decades for top earners—the percentage of Americans who don't pay income taxes has steadily risen.

In 1990, 21 percent of Americans paid no federal income taxes.[18] In 2009, it was 46 percent.[19] For nearly half of all households in America, federal government services, from the US Army to the space program, are *free*. In fact, more than half of nonpayers pay *less* than zero: 30 percent get a "refundable credit," meaning they get a check from the government for more than they paid in.[20]

Progressive tax rates at the top may not bother you, within reason. But having a lot of people with no skin in the game bothers most Americans a great deal. According to the Tax Foundation, 66 percent of Americans believe that everyone should be required to pay some amount of federal taxes.[21]

This leads to an even more troubling social democratic fact: Most Americans are on a form of welfare. The majority of Americans today consume more in government services than they pay for in taxes. When George W. Bush left office, this percentage was 60 percent. Today, it is headed toward 70 percent as various parts of President Obama's social agenda are enacted.[22]

Progressive leaders often complain that America's income distribution is lopsided—for example, that the top 5 percent of earners in America earn 35 percent of total national income. Yes, but they pay 59 percent of all the federal income taxes.[23] That is to say, their tax share is 69 percent larger than their income share.

Of course, income tax is only one part of the full tax burden Americans bear. But even if the taxes that the poor *do* pay, like payroll and excise taxes, are added in, the story is essentially unchanged. According to the CBO, adding together all federal taxes, the bottom quintile of Americans paid 4 percent of their income

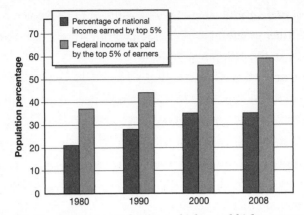

***Figure 5.2.*** *The government is loading a higher and higher percentage of the tax bill on fewer and fewer people. (Source: Gerand Prante and Mark Robyn, "Summary of Latest Federal Individual Income Tax Data," Tax Foundation Fiscal Facts, October 6, 2010, http://www.taxfoundation.org/news/show/250.html.)*

in taxes in 2007. Meanwhile the top 5 percent paid 28 percent of their income in federal taxes.[24] These large differences are explained by the high percentage of nonpayers.

Social democrats believe this is right and just because progressive taxation redistributes money and services in a way that lowers income inequality. The rest of Americans should see this as a huge problem. America simply cannot expect to maintain a responsible citizenry when half of its citizens don't pay for key public services such as the national defense.[25]

FACT #3. THE TAX AND REGULATORY BURDENS ON AMERICAN BUSINESS ARE HEAVY BY WORLD STANDARDS, AND GROWING

In social democracies, the government tends to penalize productive activity to raise revenues and achieve social goals. It does so by taking a relatively large share of private sector business revenues in taxes, and raising the cost of production through regulation. Both of these phenomena have cropped up in the United States—especially in the past few decades.

Here are two false "facts" that we often hear: (1) compared to other countries, America does not tax corporations heavily, and (2) America has a lightly regulated economy. Both are false.

Let's start with corporate taxes. The U.S. top combined statutory corporate tax rate—which includes both federal and (average) state taxes—was 39.2 percent in 2011, the second highest in the industrialized world, next only to Japan.[26]

Until the late 1980s, corporate tax rates in the social democracies exceeded America's. At that point, virtually all of the U.S. competitor nations—even the most socialist democracies such as Sweden—began to find that in order to prosper in a global marketplace, penalizing entrepreneurship in this way was unwise. To attract business, their business income tax rates began to fall. The United States lowered its top rate one time (in 1986), but never again. The U.S. even raised its top rate by 1 percentage point in 1993. Around 1990, the industrialized world average dropped below that of the U.S., and the gap has gotten wider ever since. Today, Sweden's effective corporate rate is 13 percent lower than America's.[27]

The story about regulation has followed the same pattern. Regulation has gradually increased the cost of entrepreneurial activity since about 1960. Two Lafayette University professors have calculated the current total burden of regulation on the U.S. economy, in terms of the cost of compliance.[28] They found that in 2008, the regulatory burden was $1.75 trillion. That was 12 percent of GDP—18 percent larger even than 2012's record-busting government budget deficit.[29]

The burden of regulation is especially high on small businesses, traditionally the job creators, and America's means of recovery from a national recession. In 2008, just adhering to federal rules cost businesses with nineteen workers or fewer $10,585 *per worker*. That's how much value workers need to create before employers break even and can afford to pay the first dollar in wages. Looking at the regulatory burden per employee is especially useful because it gives an idea of the drag government puts on job creation. According to one study, the burden increased by 21 percent in inflation-adjusted dollars from 2000 to 2008.[30] No wonder economists are finding that the U.S. economic recovery is so slow. Small businesses aren't hiring because it simply costs too much.

To get an idea of how much more regulated Americans' lives and the economy are today compared with the past, consider the growth in the workforce of federal regulatory agencies. In 1960, there were about 57,000 employees in this sector. Today, there are about 292,000. In 2000, the number of regulators per billion dollars of GDP was sixteen. Today, it is twenty-one.[31]

So the regulatory environment is increasingly onerous, and the U.S. taxes business more than the European countries do. This is not encouraging, if we seriously think we can avoid Europe's economic fate.

FACT #4. U.S. NATIONAL DEBT HAS GROWN STEADILY SINCE 1980, IN INFLATION-ADJUSTED TERMS.

What do Mark Twain, P.T. Barnum, and Oscar Wilde have in common? They were all wealthy people who went bankrupt. There are many similar stories: A rich celebrity lives more extravagantly than he can afford, and goes bust. Reading about his situation, you are filled with a little bit of *schadenfreude*, and a big dose of contempt. All that money, you think, and still he racked up ruinous debt. He's irresponsible.

Look in the mirror—he is you, my fellow American. As of December 2, 2011, America—the richest nation in the history of the world—owes its creditors $15,101,125,095,514.72.[32] To put that into perspective, that's $48,290 for every American, which the U.S. will either have to pay back or default on if it goes bankrupt like so many other countries throughout history.

When faced with this problem in Great Britain in the 1980s, Prime Minister Margaret Thatcher is reported to have said that the problem with socialism is that eventually you run out of other people's money. That's the road America is headed down now.

When did the binge begin? Back through history, there have been many periods of high debt, often correlated with periods of war. Eliminating those, the modern peacetime debt increases started around 1982 in America, when Ronald Reagan's defense buildups were not paid for by reducing domestic spending. Debt leveled off and decreased somewhat through the late 1990s and early 2000s, but then exploded back up to their highest levels ever, starting in 2009.

According to the Congressional Budget Office, today, our debt-to-GDP ratio is about 100 percent. The nonpartisan Congressional Budget Office estimates that by 2015 federal debt will reach 113 percent of GDP. By 2030, debt will be 194 percent of GDP.[33]

Social democracies cater to the voters by lavishing government services on them—that's their lure. Naturally this means focusing on the current generation's wants with little regard for future generations, because future generations' voters and politicians are voiceless. The inevitable result is that governments can and do begin to borrow from the future—creating the debt we see all across Europe, and increasingly right here at home.

This is not just unsustainable, foolish, and a sign of irresponsibility and poor national impulse control. It is theft from our children, and it is immoral.

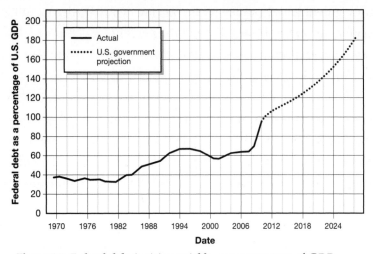

**Figure 5.3.** *Federal debt is rising quickly as a percentage of GDP. (Source: Author's calculation using Congressional Budget Office 2001 Long-Term Budget Outlook Alternative Fiscal Scenario. http://www .cbo.gov/doc.cfm?index=1221)*

FACT #5. ECONOMIC GROWTH HAS BEEN IN GENERAL
DECLINE FOR 50 YEARS.

Social democracies sacrifice robust economic growth for a strong welfare state and income equality. This statement is not controversial. Every serious economist—left or right—knows it to be true. According to an economist with the United Nations' International Labour Organization (ILO), there is a "tradeoff" that people experience "when a society has to sacrifice economic growth to achieve a reduction in inequality."[34]

Swedish economists Andreas Bergh and Magnus Henrekson have measured the negative relationship between government spending and economic growth. In a large survey of the economics literature, they found that a 10 percent increase in government spending corresponds to a decrease in economic growth of between 0.5 and 1 percentage point. In other words, if the U.S. is now growing at 2 percent per year and the federal government spends an extra $400 billion—a 10 percent increase in federal spending—expect to see economic growth move from two percent to about 1.5 percent, or even lower.[35]

Some say that it is necessary to grow government for the sake of creating jobs. But this is the reverse of the truth, according to most economists who have studied what happens to the private sector when the public sector grows. Studies vary in their conclusions, finding that every government job created eliminates between 1 and 2.2 private sector jobs. In other words, the labor effect of government growth is in the best case neutral, and in the worst case hugely destructive.[36]

Given the evidence about increases in the size of government, regulatory growth, and ballooning debt, lower economic growth over time in America is fairly predictable—and clearly present. During the 1950s and '60s, average annual growth was more than 4 percent. In the 1970s, '80s, and '90s, it was a bit over 3 percent. In the first decade of the twenty-first century, the average was 1.6 percent. The average over the last three years has been 0.1 percent.[37]

We all hope the weak growth from 2008 to the present is an historical outlier because of the recession. But we can't dismiss a broader trend: For at least fifty years, when we smooth out all the ups and downs over the business cycle, America's growth has been generally falling.[38]

Few if any economists, no matter their political views, dispute these basic trends; the data are the data. Differences in opinion only come in when we ask, "Who cares?" The social democratic position is that low growth is a cost of a comfortable, enlightened society. Basically, America is rich enough. Why go crazy trying to grow at high rates? Leave the rat race behind. Invest in social welfare. Live a little.

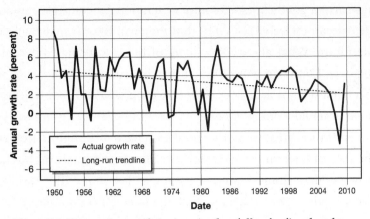

*Figure 5.4.* *Economic growth in America has fallen for five decades. (Source: "National Economic Accounts: Gross Domestic Product," Bureau of Economic Analysis, data, http://www.bea.gov/national /index.htm#gdp.)*

I encourage you to reject this viewpoint—not because you or I necessarily need to get richer, but because there are still plenty of people in our midst who do not share properly in the economy's bounty. Only strong growth will create the ecosystem to lift up whole nations and future generations. Chapter 4 showed that free enterprise's unparalleled ability to create wealth ended poverty for many millions of our own citizens and billions more around the world. This would not have occurred had we imposed policies that limited U.S. economic growth to 1 or 2 percent. It's not about *us*. It's about the *poor*. Social democracy pulls the economic ladder up behind us.

ADDED UP, the evidence is clear: America has already effectively slipped into a big government social democracy. About 40 cents of every dollar Americans earn goes to the state. The government has spent a good chunk of future generations' income too, equivalent to an entire year's GDP that they will have to pay back in the future. What about all the talk of the U.S. being "different" than the European countries? It may be true on a philosophical level, but it's not accurate when based on what the U.S. government is actually doing today.

All this is great news for those who have a European view of the role of government and do not believe free enterprise is the best system to support the U.S. culture and economy. But massive debt, stagnant growth, and high unemployment are not the American Dream for most. So it's the job of free enterprise advocates to propose an alternative model to the status quo. That starts with a practical philosophy of government, which I turn to now.

# 6

## THE GOVERNMENT WE WANT: UNCLE SAM, OR UNCLE SUGAR?

I once took a private tour of the National Palace Museum in Taiwan. This museum contains some of the most exquisite works of Chinese art in the world, transported out of mainland China in 1949 just before the country's fall to Mao Tse-tung's communists.

Almost everybody recognizes big visual differences between Western and Eastern art. I always wondered if these differences went beyond materials and technique, though—whether there was some fundamental philosophical distinction between the Western art I had been surrounded with all my life and the artistic treasures of the East. I used the opportunity that day in the museum to ask my guide what this distinction might be.

In the West, he told me, we see a blank canvas as empty, and ready to be filled up through the artist's inspiration. A painting does not exist until the artist loads the canvas with color and images.

In the East, artists don't think of creating something from nothing. They start with the belief that the finished work already exists, and simply needs the excess parts stripped away. The easiest way to understand this is not by thinking of an artist's canvas, but rather a block of stone to be sculpted. Before the artist begins, the finished sculpture exists within the block. The artist's job is to chisel away the parts that are not part of the sculpture.

The Eastern approach is useful when it comes to how we see our government.

America is a work of art, an expression of the vision of our Founders. The vision was audacious, creative, and revolutionary. But our Founders intended the work as an ongoing project. Benjamin Franklin famously promised us a republic, "If you can keep it." Every generation, the Founders knew, must work to preserve what they left us, and make it beautiful for our current generation.

For many years we have been pursuing something like the Western artistic strategy for government. We build our system up to attain what citizens and politicians demand in the moment. Every generation, we slosh more paint onto the canvas. We search for a better system by adding laws, regulations, taxes, and social engineering. The result today is garish and ugly; it bears little resemblance to the work of our Founders.

We need the art of taking things away to reveal the American Experiment within: the constitutionally limited government that allows America to be its best self. The project we need today is not a destructive one, simply tearing down the state. It is a creative one, to chisel away the statist dross that obscures our system of liberty, individual opportunity, entrepreneurship, and self-reliance.

This chapter is a description of what I think the sculpture inside the block looks like.

• • •

LEFT ON THEIR OWN, governments tend to grow. Politicians get attention—and applause—for *doing* things. When things are going poorly, people never call their congressman and scream, "Don't just do something, sit there!"

As we have seen, both Democrats and Republicans have contributed, over the decades, to the explosive expansion of the U.S. government. In order to reverse this trend, Americans need to lay out clear principles describing what the proper role of government is, and isn't. Advocating limited, constitutional government requires nerves of steel, a willingness to weather knee-jerk resistance ("You are cutting my Medicare!"), and—above all—an actual philosophy. It requires a way to answer the question of what exactly needs to be limited, reformed, and cut—and *why*.

So, as believers in the free enterprise system, what kind of government should we work toward? What does a government look like that is fair, allows people to earn success, and lifts up the downtrodden?

In his first inaugural address, Thomas Jefferson laid out his vision of "a wise and frugal Government, which shall restrain men from injuring one another, shall leave them otherwise free to regulate their own pursuits of industry and improvement, and shall not take from the mouth of labor the bread it has earned. This is the sum of good government."[1]

President Obama's vision of government is, to understate the point, a bit more expansive than Jefferson's. The U.S. government, in his view, should be judged on whether or not "it helps families find jobs at a decent wage, health care they can afford, a retirement that is dignified."[2] In a bit over 200 years, we have moved from a president who believes the purpose of government is to leave you free to live your life as you see fit, to a president who thinks that the state is included in finding you a job, getting you a doctor, ensuring you save for your retirement, and a long list of other things.

What philosophy of government preserves Jefferson's ethos, while recognizing that the world has changed in dramatic ways? In my view, America would do well to turn to the wisdom of German-born economist and Nobel laureate Friedrich Hayek. Hayek's classic book *The Road to Serfdom*, written in 1944, is obligatory reading for all advocates of free enterprise—and still provides an excellent guide to the role of government.

Conservatives admire and quote Hayek incessantly. What's surprising to some is that he taught that the government, for moral as well as efficiency reasons, can and should provide a minimum basic safety net for citizens. And like most other economists, he also believed it should address "market failures." But that's all—and that is dramatically less than what the government currently does.

LET'S BEGIN WITH the idea of the minimum safety net, since the easiest—and most frequently cited—criticism of the free enterprise movement is that its proponents want to instate a purely Darwinian society, in which the weakest members are left on their own, without any support from the government. In 2011, President Obama said this of his political opponents: "Their philosophy is simple: we are better off when everyone is left to fend for themselves and play by their own rules."[3]

I have almost never heard conservatives and free enterprise advocates make such a preposterous claim. Most believe that it is appropriate for the government to provide *some* safety net for its citizens. Most are very comfortable providing some minimal standard of living in terms of food, shelter, and medical care.

Even hardline conservatives don't object to minimum basic protections for poor people, provided publicly, in some cases (and, in others, by private charities). Demagogues who accuse the political right of wanting to throw the poor out into the snow are not just exaggerating: they're simply wrong.

Still, most free enterprise advocates—and most Americans in general—believe that the government has gone too far and is mollycoddling the citizenry. A February 2009 Fox News poll shows that 76 percent of Americans believe that we now rely too much on the government and not enough on ourselves. Only 20 percent disagree with that sentiment.[4]

The basic problem is that America's minimum "safety net" has become appallingly broad. It has little to do with helping the poor, and a lot to do with passing out favors to voters and smoothing the risks out of ordinary life. For example, we often hear that Social Security is part of a basic safety net. But as currently configured, the program is in large part a benefit to middle-class people, especially the majorities that have taken more out of the system than they ever put into it. Similarly, Medicare Part D (subsidizing prescription drugs to seniors) is not part of the safety net for the poor per se; it is a $62 billion benefit that is consumed by a group that is made up primarily of middle-class Americans.[5]

The job of a social safety net starts with an answer to this question: What is an unacceptable standard of living in America? In my view, it is unacceptable for someone in America's wealthy society to go without access to basic medical care, sufficient food, and basic shelter. Pretty uncontroversial, I think.

But the safety net is *not* a means to increase material equality, a way to take any but the most grievous risks out of life, a way to pass out rewards to groups based on demographics or political clout, or a source of benefits to the middle class.

So Medicaid for people below poverty is an appropriate function of the safety net: We can and should find a way to cap its costs and preserve it, as the next chapter will detail. But the government subsidizing prescription drugs for all seniors (not just the poorest) is simply a favor to a key voting bloc, and European-style health coverage is a move toward social democracy. Food aid programs for the indigent are part of the safety net, but agricultural subsidies to prop up farmers' incomes are not. Homeless shelters are part of the safety net, but housing programs that serve the middle class like rent control and government flood insurance are not. A guaranteed minimum Social Security benefit that lifts seniors to the poverty line is part of the safety net, but paying anyone who is not poor any more than they paid in (plus a reasonable rate of return) is not.

The true safety net includes programs like food stamps so the poor can eat, Temporary Assistance for Needy Families (TANF) for low-income families with small children, Medicaid, and Supplemental Security Income (SSI) for the indigent and disabled. These federal programs are not cheap—together, family support, food assistance, Medicaid, and SSI totaled $432 billion in 2010 (a bit less than 3 percent of the GDP and 8.5 percent of the 2010 federal budget)—but they are a defensible safety net for the disadvantaged.[6]

The government could eliminate waste from these programs and spend less than it currently does. Moreover, welfare reform in the 1990s showed that these programs should never be designed as a permanent source of support, because that hurts the poor and their children. But few people, including few conservatives and free marketeers, really want to kill these programs and substitute nothing for them. The safety net—continuously improved and reformed—should continue to be there for the neediest of citizens.

Clearly, reasonable people can disagree on what "poor" means and what an "acceptable standard" for them is. But I believe that is the debate we should have, not a debate about whether the current out-of-control entitlement system—which largely benefits the nonpoor—should continue.

THE SECOND AREA of legitimate government activity is "market failure"—specific cases in which free markets don't function on their own to create efficient outcomes. Since Adam Smith published *The Wealth of Nations*, nearly all economists have agreed that such circumstances *can* justify some degree of state intervention in the system—not to weaken free enterprise, but to strengthen it.

There are four sources of market failure: monopolies, externalities, public goods, and information asymmetries.

## MONOPOLIES

A monopoly is, literally, "one seller." Monopolies are all around us. The corner bakery is technically one, as the only seller of bread on that corner, but its monopoly status poses no problem because there are other bakers on other blocks. A more worrisome monopoly is the only seller of an entire product. For example, until 1983, the phone company in America, AT&T—known back then as "Ma Bell"—was the only provider of long-distance phone service. It was horrendously expensive. (When I was a child, I remember my father sweating bullets because my mother was on a long-distance call to my aunt who lived in the next state *for nearly an hour*. Today, my kids don't even know what a "long-distance call" is.)

There are several problems with monopolies. In general, the lack of competition means prices tend to be high, service tends to be poor, entrepreneurs are unable to deliver innovation to consumers, and companies spend an inordinate amount of money lobbying government to maintain the one-seller privilege.

Monopolies like Ma Bell are a threat to economic prosperity and the good of citizens. When a company can establish a monopoly by forming barriers to competition, the company may prosper, but the citizenry won't; thus the government's interest in this market failure. The famous case of Standard Oil's monopoly pricing schemes of the 1880s led to the Sherman Antitrust Act of 1890, which most economists still today regard as beneficial and prudent regulation.

A related phenomenon is price fixing through the collusion of competitors, which makes an effective joint monopoly. Adam Smith wryly explained: "People of the same trade seldom meet together, even for merriment and diversion, but the conversation ends in a conspiracy against the public, or in some contrivance to raise prices."[7] Manipulating a competitive market through collusion is a legitimate area of attention for government regulators. That is why it is illegal for the CEO of United Airlines to call his counterpart at Delta to talk about the prices they should charge.

These rules are not absolute, however. There are times when a monopoly makes sense—for instance, when it protects intellectual property. If you invent something, you get a patent or trademark that protects you from others who might steal your idea. If Amgen develops a new drug that cures a disease, the government says Amgen has several years to sell it without competition from generic substitutes. Microsoft has the legal right to be the only company that can use its brand and logo. Lady Gaga owns the legal rights to her songs and gets paid if you want to perform them professionally. In these cases, the government is correct in protecting monopoly power. If it did not, few would have an incentive to innovate.

Unfortunately, we should not assume that when it comes to monopoly policies, the government will sort out the "good" from the "bad" monopolies and make policy accordingly. Governments have been known to leave intellectual property unprotected, protect predatory monopolies, and even set them up in order to make money at the expense of the general public.

Remember the last time you tried to find a New York City taxi in the rain? It took twenty minutes because the city government, which sells exclusive licenses ("medallions"), limits the number of taxis to below competitive levels. Currently, the price of an individual taxi medallion—the license for one taxicab—in New York is $696,000 on the open market.[8] That's to buy the right to sell a product where competition is legally restricted in what is truly a conspiracy against the consumer.

Sometimes, the government itself operates a monopoly. In many countries, for instance, the government is the sole provider of land-line telephone service. Inevitably, it is an expensive and ghastly service—maybe even worse than Ma Bell. I lived in Spain when the government still owned the Spanish phone monopoly, *Telefónica*. Everything about it was a nightmare—people waited for months to get a new phone line, the service was miserable, and it was expensive. Why did the Spanish government own *Telefónica*? Because it was a huge cash cow and, basically, just another tax on citizens.

There are plenty of similar government monopolies in America. Does your state have a lottery? You might say it's just good clean fun, and it's better to have the government running it than a bunch of private-sector hoodlums. Think again. Private casinos have a profit margin of just a few cents on the dollar. Meanwhile, the average state government lottery pays just 52 cents for every dollar it takes in.[9] Lower-income citizens typically purchase lottery tickets; a National Bureau of Economic Research study shows that they finance the tickets largely by reducing their expenditures on necessities like housing and food.[10] The state lottery is nothing more than a government monopoly that exploits the poor and vulnerable.

So the bottom line on monopolies is that they are a source of market failure, but not in a straightforward or simple way. Sometimes, a monopoly is clearly predatory and bad; sometimes, it leads to better outcomes than competition. The right guide to regulating a monopoly should be, "What is best for the consumer?" not, "What will protect powerful industries?" nor, "What will generate the most revenues for the government?"

Unfortunately, when it comes to monopolies, the government has generally not proved itself competent or reliable in protecting the public interest.

## EXTERNALITIES

Years ago when I was working on my PhD, my wife and I were living in a small apartment in a college town. I was studying a hundred hours a week and under a lot of stress. The one thing I really craved was a good night's sleep. Unfortunately, there were a lot of undergraduates in our neighborhood who were studying little, and partying a lot. Every Friday and Saturday, and many Sundays through Thursdays, our neighbors (the twelve guys living next door) made the most of their freedom, all night long. That meant lots of noise—and no sleep for me.

This problem was what economists call an "externality." Externalities are things that affect your well-being outside the realm of prices and free markets. A classic case—and obviously a more important one than my lack of sleep—is unabated pollution. A chemical company pours junk into a river without any law to stop it, destroying the river's life and beauty. Markets may not work to solve the problem, and it may be appropriate to pass a law saying the factory can't do that. Or in the case of my partying neighbors, many college towns have passed laws against having raucous keggers out on the porch between 10 p.m. and 6 a.m.

Externalities make markets fail, and that is why governments might legitimately pay attention to them. But government action is not the only way to solve externalities. The free market in many cases can solve this market failure even more efficiently. The economist Ronald Coase won a Nobel Prize in economics by showing that private bargaining works at least as well as government action to solve externality problems, if property rights are clearly defined.[11] So instead of a law saying a factory can't pollute the river, the law can assign the property rights over the river to the neighbors, who can then make their own decision—or even bargain with the factory owner so he has to pay them if he wants to pollute. This idea is known as the "Coase Theorem."

There are many cases in which the Coase Theorem has efficiently solved externality problems far better than government command-and-control. For example, few communities want a noisy airport in their midst. They often work simply to make all airport construction illegal, posing a huge problem in an era of expanding air travel. Some communities, however, have used their property rights to negotiate with airlines in reaching a win-win solution to price the noise of planes arriving and departing. They simply charge airlines more to land noisy planes at odd hours, and the landing fees go to the community. A noisy old DC9 arriving at midnight costs far more to land than a new 747 with a noise muffler arriving at noon.[12]

The Coase Theorem has informal implications as well. I grew up in a neighborhood where many people didn't take care of their property. The woman who lived across the street had grass so long it looked like a field of wheat. (Another family on the block was raising chickens in their living room, but at least we didn't have to look at that.) My parents thought about filing some sort of complaint, but they quickly figured out that our neighbor had the right to cut her grass or not, as she saw fit. So they solved the externality problem privately: They told my brother and me to cut her grass while she was at work, convincing us that maybe she'd be grateful and pay us later. (She didn't—and we were lucky she didn't call the cops on us for trespassing.)

Externalities can be positive, too. Beekeepers create a positive externality for farmers whose crops are pollinated by the bees. Similarly, I get a benefit for free—a positive externality—from living in a neighborhood today where the other families are decent and considerate and the kids are a good influence on mine. (Maybe they say the same about us, but I won't swear to that.)

A policy-relevant example of a positive externality is that of companies locating in a city or state and creating jobs. One of Texas's claims to fame is that it is home to sixty-four Fortune 500 companies, the most of any state.[13] Many of these companies, which moved to Texas from other parts of the country, were drawn by more than just good ol' Texas hospitality. The state offers a low-tax, low-litigation, low-union environment in return for the enormous positive externalities to the state that come from the 328,000 new jobs created between June 2009 and July 2011 (47 percent of all net job growth in the U.S. over that period).[14]

Like monopolies, externalities seem simple, until you dig in a little. Some are positive, and some are negative. Some can best be solved by the government, while others are best left alone. And as in the case of monopolies, the government has a poor record when it comes to dealing appropriately with this market failure.

## Public Goods

When I was a kid, the local Catholic archbishop was a famous antiwar activist. One of his public gestures against the American military industrial complex was to refuse to pay part of his income taxes to protest the United States' continued involvement in the nuclear arms race.[15] He felt he should not have to pay for a part of the government that he did not value.

What would happen if everybody did that? Say the IRS Form 1040 were changed to let you pay whatever you thought the army and other services were worth to you. Would you pay $500? $1,000? To defend the nation at the current level, the average American would have to pay $2,462 for national defense.[16] Assuming most Americans wouldn't pay that, what would happen to the national defense? What would happen to everyone's safety?

Maybe you think the U.S. spends far too much on defense, so spending less would be just fine. If so, then apply the same reasoning to the police department or the roads system. Imagine if the government went house to house asking people for contributions to keep the bridges safe. Are you ready to try your luck on the Golden Gate Death Trap?

National defense, police, fire protection, and many other things are public goods. They are things we want and need, but which we can't practically exclude people from using if they don't pay.[17] For example, my archbishop refused to pay for the army, but he was still protected from foreign aggressors, just like the rest of us. In contrast, a "private good"—like a donut or a pencil—is excludable. If you don't pay for it, you can't have it.

Public goods can make markets fail, because private sellers will underprovide them when people refuse to pay. So the government doesn't fund them that way. Instead, it taxes citizens and pays for the public goods at a level that reflects public demand. It's a grand public bargain. We all recognize we want things like the police, but we don't trust ourselves or our neighbors to fund them voluntarily—so we all agree to pay, just as long as everybody else has to pay as well.

Of course, there's a dark side to this system: everyone has an opportunity to claim that his or her favorite hobbyhorse is a "public good" and needs public money. Public television? A public good, we're told—despite the lack of public demand—and thus in need of public money. Offensive art? Another public good, even if millions might say instead that it's a public *bad*. I might as well shove my way to the public trough and argue that this *book* is a public good, because America needs a strong defense of the free enterprise system, but people are simply not buying my book in sufficient quantities. Bail *me* out, Uncle Sugar!

In other words, the definition of a public good is clear, but the list of them is not. The concept is constantly abused, and government resources are wasted as a result.

## INFORMATION ASYMMETRIES

Imagine that shortly after moving to a new town, your refrigerator breaks down. Not knowing anyone in town, you randomly call a repair shop. Are you worried? Probably, if you, like me, know nothing about refrigerators. The repairman can tell you almost anything is wrong with your refrigerator ("Your D-57 hoses are all shot. I see it all the time on these models. It's gonna be about 400 bucks."), and you won't know if it is true or not. So all you can hope for is his honesty—or sufficient licensing and threat of sanctions from the government to dissuade him from cheating you.

This is a case of what economists call an "information asymmetry": where one side of a market has more information than the other and chooses to exploit the difference. In the example, the information asymmetry leads to worry and maybe an inconvenience. In the worse case, it can make markets melt down entirely. Economist George Akerlof won a Nobel Prize in economics for analyzing information asymmetries in a famous essay entitled, "The Market for 'Lemons.'"[18] He took the example of used cars, in which the dealer knows the lemons from the good cars, but buyers don't, and showed that the whole market can stop functioning as a result. On average, a car's price will be higher than a lemon is worth, but less than a good car is worth. Sellers thus have an incentive to increase the number of lemons (which turn a profit), while buyers are less and less able to afford a good car at a fair price. Slowly but surely, Akerlof showed, the lemons will dominate, and the market will dissolve.

Lemons can be people as well as cars, as every insurance company knows. One chronic information asymmetry problem is that the people who most want health insurance are those who are already sick. Insurance can't work this way because companies lose money on the sick and earn their profits on customers who *don't* get sick. If the sick are the majority buying the insurance, the rates will skyrocket, chasing away the healthy and wrecking the market.

Scandals and corruption on Wall Street are basically asymmetric information problems. A person or group trading with inside information means they know something the rest of the market doesn't. They trade on that and take profits at the expense of the uninformed.

The government can help in these situations. Policy makers can make it illegal to pass off a lemon as a good car by hiding problems. They can make it illegal for a person to tell a health insurance company that he's well when he is actually sick. They can require money-back guarantees or recourse to the attorney general when a product turns out to be defective. Similarly, the public sector can and should prohibit insider trading and many other financial market predations.

The government doesn't need to sort out all information asymmetries, however. In many cases, the private sector can do so instead. Money-back guarantees became commonplace in the retail sector in the 1960s, after high-quality companies realized that the guarantees would give them a competitive advantage by signaling to customers that they could be trusted. Car companies compete by offering better warranties than their competitors. Insurance companies require health exams before writing life insurance policies. (One hundred years ago, insurance companies were even more ingenious: Before elevators were common, health insurers would locate their offices on the upper floors of buildings and require prospective policy buyers to sign their policies at the office, in person. The idea was that if a prospective client could make it up all those stairs, he was probably healthy enough to be insured.)

Information asymmetries are a legitimate area of government involvement in the economy. But regulation is not the only—or sometimes, the best—way to solve the problem.

IN SUMMARY, there are four big sources of market failure. Sometimes markets fail; sometimes they don't. Sometimes governments fix market failure problems by intervening; sometimes they try and fail; sometimes they make things worse, by accident or on purpose. When should the government act?

To justify government intervention in a market, several things must be evident. A source of market failure must be clearly present. It must involve a monopoly, a negative externality, a public good, or asymmetric information. Many government policies fail at exactly this stage. For example, President Obama claims the housing crisis was due to an information asymmetry in the form of "mortgage lenders that tricked families into buying homes they couldn't afford."[19] But does anybody *not* know that prices of homes can both rise and fall? Or whether they can make a mortgage payment on their current wage? We all know that mortgage contracts are complicated, but is it really reasonable to blame lenders and markets, instead of a lack of common sense and personal responsibility?

What about the so-called monopolistic health insurance companies and the need to regulate the price of coverage? Insurance companies are not monopolies; they face fierce competition. If Aetna doesn't offer what consumers want, charges prices that are uncompetitively high, or has lousy service, another insurer will welcome their business. (That is, unless the government regulations have already wiped out the private markets, as has happened in some places.)

A favorite "public good" of President Obama is high-speed rail. It will supposedly revolutionize the transit system and benefit everyone but people won't pay for it privately—so it requires federal subsidies. Actually, people don't want to pay for it because it isn't particularly useful and thus is not a public good. The projects that the government plans to subsidize include a $715 million project to build a hundred miles of track between the small towns of Borden and Corcoran, California, and a "high-speed" train from Iowa City that will take longer to get to Chicago than the bus does today.[20]

Let's say there *is* a source of market failure, though. That isn't enough by itself. The market also has to be *failing* in practice. There are many, many cases in which there is a source of market failure but the market works just fine, because people solve the problems themselves, without any government action at all. I've already discussed a few private-sector mechanisms that solve market failures, such as private warranties. But even more obvious is that people avoid many market failures just by being decent.

Honest businesspeople want to prosper honestly, not by cheating consumers or using predatory business tactics, even if they could get away with these things. Decent people refrain all the time from creating burdensome externalities on others (that is why you listen to the Bee Gees in your car with the windows rolled up). And most Americans do their part to provide public goods privately when they give to charity.[21] Americans have a whole system for dealing privately with market failures so they don't have to rely so much on the government. It's called "social capital," the subject of the next section of this chapter.

Still, some market failures persist. Does this mean the government should definitely act? No, not unless the state can actually solve the problem, and solve it cost effectively.

Many market failures are irremediable by government at a reasonable price. The externality of traffic noise bothers me in my office while I'm trying to work. Can the government fix this? Not without measures in which the costs would dramatically outweigh the benefits.

The same goes for the tangled web of new economic regulations created over the past few years. Remember the Consumer Protection Act of 2010 (also known as "Dodd-Frank"), which weighed in at 848 pages of legislation intended to prevent market

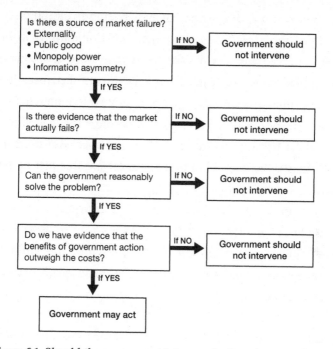

***Figure 6.1.*** *Should the government intervene in the private market?*

failures like those that created the recent financial crisis? It was enacted ostensibly to sort out information asymmetries between informed financiers and the uninformed public. But it flunks the test of government intervention. According to the evidence so far, the law won't prevent another crisis and the regulations will cost more than they save.[22]

All together, these justifications set a high bar for government involvement in the private economy. Figure 6.1 shows the conditions that have to be met before government should act.

The point of Figure 6.1 is that a great deal of what the government does *sounds* sensible, but it is not. In providing a minimum safety net or addressing market failures, the government wastes resources or tries to do things it cannot achieve cost effectively.

Even worse, much government activity doesn't even try to solve market failures or provide a safety net. In the modern *adlibocracy*, what passes for governing philosophy is little more than a bromide such as, "The government should do nice things for people." Today, the government's spending binge is largely directed toward rewarding political friends (like public-sector unions), social engineering (see ObamaCare's mandates or the housing policies that led to the current crisis), and good old-fashioned pork (look almost anywhere in the economic stimulus spending).

In the end, much of government that purports to enhance people's lives actually makes things worse for citizens and keeps them sliding toward a system they don't want. And ultimately, it helps explain why eight in ten are dissatisfied with the democratically elected government.

IF THE GOVERNMENT does its job—which is to say, refrains from acting in most cases—many market failures will go unsolved by the public sector. Principled politicians will have to tell citizens that they know things aren't perfect, but it isn't prudent for the government to step in, because it can't solve the problem—at least not in a way that uses tax dollars cost effectively.

This does not mean people can't promote other solutions, though. A dangerous progressive fallacy is that if the government doesn't solve a market failure, it will always remain unsolved. Without publicly funded trains, for instance, transportation will be inadequate. Without stringent laws, honest people will become criminals. Without money for public broadcasting, people will have no access to high-quality radio, and so on. This is ridiculous.

To resolve many actual market failures, people don't need the government at all. They need well-functioning markets, of course.

But they also need voluntary action and a healthy culture in which people do things for each other without being forced or bribed by the state. People need what scholars call "social capital," which is the trust and social cohesiveness that promote voluntary activity to meet challenges in civil society.

Trust and cohesion in healthy neighborhoods and communities make life easier, more pleasant, less bureaucratic, and more efficient.[23] In high-trust societies, it is easier to conduct business and requires fewer resources in policing and the adjudication of disputes. There is less cheating, corruption, and crime. And where there are a lot of civic institutions, people help each other for mutual benefit.

More specifically, where social capital is plentiful, people are more likely to refrain from making excess noise or letting their property deteriorate (circumventing externalities). Many minor business deals between friends require nothing but a handshake, and people don't take advantage of each other (avoiding an information asymmetry problem). If a person sees something suspicious at a neighbor's house, he goes to check on it (a public good). In all these cases, individuals are better suited than governments to solve the market failure at hand, but they require a climate of trust and voluntary action.[24]

Social capital is what encourages someone to refrain from exploiting an information asymmetry by giving back the change if a cashier gives her too much. It induces her to give to charities that provide public goods for people she won't ever meet. It holds her back from creating externalities in traffic with obnoxious driving. Every day, social capital solves small and large market failures that government can't and shouldn't address.

It is easy to see how important social capital is to people's lives. Yet strangely, until recently there were few good measures of this important quality of life issue. In response to this, researchers at several universities and foundations around the United States undertook in 2000 to measure social capital with a survey. They asked tens of thousands of citizens about their levels of trust, charity, and community involvement. Dozens of American communities were represented, from rural areas to big cities.

The results were fairly predictable: In small communities where people know their neighbors, social capital is high. In big, anonymous cities, social capital is low. For example, on an index of social trust, big cities like Chicago, Boston, and Los Angeles are near the bottom with a score of 81. The two top communities are Bismarck, North Dakota (131) and rural South Dakota (150).[25]

How do people experience these differences in everyday life today? Try driving in Chicago after a few weeks in North Dakota, and compare how others treat you. Where are you more likely to get mugged—Irene, South Dakota, or downtown Los Angeles? And if you move into a new home in downtown Boston, your neighbors might not welcome you with a fresh-baked pie. In modern America, big cities are great if you want a good restaurant or to see the opera. They're lousy for social capital.[26]

IN THE 1830S, what impressed Alexis de Tocqueville most about America was the astonishingly high levels of social capital. Probably the most famous passage in Tocqueville's classic *Democracy in America* addresses this point:

> Americans of all ages, all conditions, and all disposi-
> tions constantly form associations. . . . The Americans
> make associations to give entertainments, to found
> seminaries, to build inns, to construct churches, to

diffuse books, to send missionaries to the antipodes;
in this manner they found hospitals, prisons, and
schools. If it is proposed to inculcate some truth or to
foster some feeling by the encouragement of a great
example, they form a society. Wherever at the head of
some new undertaking you see the government in
France, or a man of rank in England, in the United
States you will be sure to find an association.[27]

This was, in Tocqueville's mind, the secret to American success.
In the eyes of a twenty-first-century social scientist, Tocqueville
was simply observing the fact that social capital solved market
failures that government couldn't address, given America's sparse
population and ungovernable frontier. It would have been impossible to tax the population sufficiently to fund government hospitals
and schools in, say, 1830s rural Nebraska. America was successful
because a new nation of social entrepreneurs took these tasks upon
themselves. In the process, they built strong communities of trust,
reliant on themselves and not on the government. This is the
legacy of freedom and limited government that Americans still say
they love.

The links between social capital and America's success have
been evident to social scientists for many years. In one study in the
1950s, the American political scientist Edward Banfield spent a
year in a small, poor town in southern Italy.[28] His vivid observa-
tions formed the basis for his book *The Moral Basis of a Backward
Society*, in which he laid out the evidence that the town was
impoverished because the people did not recognize or reward
meritorious behavior, had little sense of fair play, and no sense of
charity toward one another.[29] He noted, for instance, that the local
orphanage in the town was run by nuns in a crumbling medieval

monastery. No one in the town gave a lira for its support, and not even unemployed stone masons volunteered to help in its upkeep—even though all the orphans came from the town itself.

Banfield forcefully made his point by comparing the Italian town with a comparably sized—but prosperous—little town in Utah. On one random day, the local newspaper in the Utah town contained mentions of dozens of voluntary charitable projects and activities. The local church had just raised $1,393.11 in pennies for a children's hospital 350 miles away; there was a Red Cross membership drive going on; a circus was being held to raise money for a new dormitory at the local junior college; there were meetings all over town of the Parent Teacher Association (PTA).

There are many market failures that social capital cannot solve—either that the government can and should address (for example, the public good of military power) or that may simply go unsolved (such as externalities from differences in religious practices). But social capital is an important component of a healthy nation.

Unfortunately, some experts believe social capital is generally in decline in America. Harvard political scientist Robert Putnam wrote a bestselling book in 2000 entitled *Bowling Alone*, in which he argued that people's trust in each other and tendency to participate voluntarily in their communities has plummeted in recent decades. Not all experts agree, but clearly Putnam's claim resonates with millions of Americans who have seen evidence around them of eroding social networks and falling trust in their communities.

Quite reasonably, Putnam laid the blame for falling social capital on phenomena such as television and urbanization. But there is more to it. The rise of statism described in the last chapter is also a key reason for the slide away from the self-governing ideals that Tocqueville found so striking. The voluntary sector falls as the public sector grows and takes over more functions in people's lives. More of life is identified as a competency of the government, and thus not the responsibility of individuals.

This is not just conjecture, but demonstrable truth. In dozens of studies, economists have shown that government funding "crowds out" voluntary contributions of both money and time to charities.[30] This stands to reason. If the government is supporting something, people don't "need" to. Furthermore, people will be less likely to ask for help: One major research finding is that non-profits quickly conform to government support and spend less time and effort fund-raising.[31]

This pattern is not innocuous when it comes to a flourishing nation. Government insinuates itself into more and more corners of people's lives, alienating them from each other and their communities. It obviates what philosopher Edmund Burke called the "little platoons" of ordinary life, which create meaning in a way the government never can or will. That is the conclusion of a great deal of research.[32] It is also the essence of an entire philosophical and religious principle called *subsidiarity*, which teaches that in order to help people thrive, matters ought to be handled by the smallest, lowest, or least centralized authority.[33] If the family can solve the problem, don't call on the city. If the city can solve it, don't call on the state. And so on.

In other words, if people are to flourish, they need incentives and the ability to help each other voluntarily. In many cases, this amounts to keeping the government out, even if things aren't perfect.

I AM CLEARLY MAKING A CASE for government that is far more circumscribed than the government in America today. A state that restricts itself to minimum basic standards for the poor, and sorting out market failures cost effectively, is in stark contrast to today's exploding public sector. The sculpture is much smaller than the block that currently contains it.

In this chapter, I have tried to explain *what* I believe the government should and shouldn't do. And we already know the *why*: to allow free enterprise's moral promises to help the greatest number of people flourish. Still, we need to get down to specifics and identify the actual policies Americans care most about and the ways in which we can make them into an expression of our values. That is our task for the next chapter.

# 7

## Winning the Moral Debate on the Policy Issues That Matter Most to Americans

One recent afternoon, a congressman friend of mine called with an unusual request. He knew I was writing a book about how to win the fight for free enterprise. He knew all my arguments about earned success, meritocratic fairness, and lifting up the poor. However, he wanted advice on something more specific: how to make the best possible moral argument for a particular tax policy that was about to come before Congress.

As the president of a think tank, I'm used to giving answers to specific policy questions. What is the right income exclusion so that a flat tax is not regressive? What is the economic multiplier on military spending? What leads to better growth in an economy—cutting government spending or raising taxes? But I have rarely had a policymaker ask me how to construct the moral argument for a specific policy. That's a very different challenge from making the moral argument for free enterprise as a whole. A huge philosophical exegesis about the morality of freedom won't have the right effect. It would be like reciting *Paradise Lost* at a limerick competition.

To argue specific policies, free enterprise advocates need to be fluent in the moral case and make it in just a few sentences. We need to follow it with the relevant facts and data, and offer practical principles for good governance. And we need to have the specific policy proposals that are consistent with the moral case. In this chapter, I will demonstrate this process and make the argument in the case of five domestic economic policy issues Americans are most concerned about today.

What are these issues? If you listen to the pundits, you might think that most Americans are fixated on "wedge" issues like illegal immigration and gay marriage. There are shrill proponents on both sides of these issues that make for great TV. But in reality, when Americans shut off the TV and sit around the kitchen table to talk, they aren't mostly concerned with these issues. Over many years, polls have repeatedly revealed that when it comes to domestic policy, Americans are primarily concerned with a core set of topics, almost all of which revolve around economics.

A June 2011 CNN poll listed a large number of policy issues and asked people to evaluate how important each would be to their vote for president.[1] The most important issues were, in order: the economy, unemployment, health care, the deficit, gas prices, terrorism, taxes, and the Medicare entitlement. Five of the top eight issues focus directly on economics, and two of the other three are closely related. To be relevant to American voters, these are the issues advocates of free enterprise must be ready to address, morally and practically.

In the following sections, I will focus on most of these important issues with structured arguments on the subjects of economic growth, jobs and unemployment, deficits and debt, entitlements, and taxes. Obviously, in just a few pages, I won't pretend to give readers a truly comprehensive policy treatment. Whole books have been written on each topic. Nonetheless, each section serves as an example of how to build a policy argument in a way that will arm those sympathetic to the free enterprise viewpoint and persuade (or at least gently confront) those who are not.

Each argument follows a specific outline: First, I start with the brief moral case for policy reform. This is not a long treatise on the morality of every issue, but rather the "elevator speech" for the *why* of each policy, highlighting the basic moral points I believe are essential to address before moving on to the *what*.

Second, I present salient evidence that makes the case that policy change or reform is necessary. This evidence is generally quite counterintuitive, not because I am searching for surprises per se, but because if the facts were intuitive, reform would already have taken place.

Third, I offer what I believe are the basic principles for better policy. I have found these to be the guideposts to improvement in each policy area. As circumstances change, these principles will not.

Finally, I lay out the actual policies I think are currently most necessary and constructive. The policies I propose are some of those my AEI colleagues and I have worked on most intensively, have offered to presidential candidates and in congressional testimony, and which we believe should be part of any broader set of policy solutions.[2]

## ISSUE I: GETTING THE U.S. ECONOMY GROWING AGAIN

First off, we have to make the moral case for economic growth. But economic growth isn't "moral," right? Wrong. In the words of Harvard economist Benjamin Friedman, "Economic growth . . .

fosters greater opportunity, tolerance of diversity, social mobility, commitment to fairness, and dedication to democracy."[3] All of these things have deep moral implications.

Weak economic growth means the end of the opportunity society in America. Your grandparents believed your parents could do better than they did; your parents wanted the same for you. That's how the American Dream works, and it is not fair to steal that legacy from our children by consuming tomorrow's growth today in the form of exploding government and lavish entitlements we can't afford.

Furthermore, weak growth disproportionately hurts those who most need new economic opportunities: the poor. The world experienced effectively no economic growth for millennia, and then saw explosive growth due to capitalism. This has literally saved billions of people from brutish poverty. But there is more to do, here in America and around the world. To fulfill the moral promises of the pursuit of happiness, basic fairness, and help for the less fortunate, America's economy must continue to grow.

Here are some essential facts to help people understand why better policies are needed to stimulate growth:

- America's growth is spiraling downward, just like growth in the European countries. From 1950 to 2000, the U.S. averaged 3.6 percent real annual GDP growth. For the last ten years, GDP has grown at an annual rate of 1.7 percent. Since the recession began in 2007, U.S. growth has fallen to 0.1 percent.[4]

- Many economists believe our natural growth rate is now too low to pull the U.S. out of its economic malaise and solve its fiscal crisis. Even to lower the budget deficit to 5 percent of GDP, America would need to achieve a year-on-year growth rate of at least 4 percent.[5]

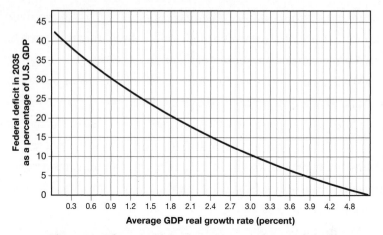

***Figure 7.1.*** *What would it take to grow our way out of our problems? Growth rates needed today to lower the 2035 projected budget deficit. (Source: Author's calculations. Congressional Budget Office 2011 Long-Term Budget Outlook Alternative Fiscal Scenario. http://www.cbo.gov /doc.cfm?index=12212.)*

• Growth today means a better life for the future. Every 1 percent of additional growth today will double real incomes seventy-two years from now.[6]

There are two contradictory and irreconcilable strategies for achieving higher economic growth in the U.S., and Americans must choose which one they want to pursue.

According to the first, the key to restarting economic growth is the state. The policy prescription is therefore higher levels of government—more stimulus, more taxes, and more borrowing.

According to the second strategy, the source of economic growth is free enterprise. The policy prescription is to get government out of the way of entrepreneurs. That means tax reform, less government spending, and policies that make it easier for entrepreneurs to succeed.

If we choose the second strategy, there is just one basic principle to remember in making policy: Break down barriers to entrepreneurship. The president should wake up each morning and—before his feet hit the floor—ask, "What will I do today to get the government out of the way of entrepreneurs?"

WITH A MORAL IMPERATIVE firmly in mind, and armed with both the key facts and fundamental principle for economic growth, what specific policy measures should we advocate?

Fixing the tax code is a top priority—America's tax system is a huge barrier to entrepreneurship. At a minimum, the U.S. should drop the top federal corporate income tax rate to no more than 25 percent, from the current 35 percent, which is internationally uncompetitive. As for individuals, the U.S. should replace the current income tax with a consumption tax to stop discouraging investment. These reforms would spur growth significantly, according to the best nonpartisan estimates available.[7] More specifics on each of these policies will come a bit later in the chapter.

In addition to fixing the tax code, the U.S. should also lower regulatory barriers to business. Examples of onerous regulation have been easy to find for years. But most recently and prominently, the Obama Administration's regulatory response to the financial crisis—the Dodd-Frank Act—created huge new sets of damaging rules for companies large and small. Yet no evidence suggests it will do anything to prevent another economic calamity.[8]

But shouldn't we do something to prevent another housing and financial crisis? Yes, and that means facing up to what really went wrong in the American economy. The housing crisis occurred because people borrowed too much to buy houses, with down payments that were too low. Without a sufficient down payment, people had an incentive to walk away from their mortgages when their home values fell below what they owed—and millions walked away as a simple business decision during the 2008–2009 recession.

To mitigate the risk of another collapse of this sort, America doesn't need 848 pages of legislation. It needs a government that stops encouraging people with subsidized mortgages and tax deductions to buy houses they cannot afford. And on the private sector side, lenders could simply require a 20 percent down payment on any residential housing loan. A 20 percent down payment requirement would ensure that every homeowner had enough invested to forbear most housing price downturns without walking away. It would do more to prevent the next collapse than the myriad regulations of the Dodd-Frank Act, and would do so without hindering growth.

In addition to tax cuts and regulatory reform, growth requires that government spending be capped and cut. The current administration argues that government spending can stimulate long-term growth, but this claim is inconsistent with the evidence. Chapter 5 showed that a 10 percent increase in government spending and taxation has the effect of reducing economic growth by up to 1 percentage point per year.[9]

There are three reasons government spending hampers growth. First, spending that is paid for with current taxes creates a drag on the private economy. Second, if spending is paid for by borrowing, this lowers the confidence of investors today who know that sooner or later it will have to be paid back. Third, when borrowed money is ultimately paid back, the taxes hurt growth in those future years.

Later in the chapter, I'll single out specific areas of government spending that need to be cut: entitlements and the government payroll, in particular. But for now, it suffices to say that out-of-control government spending is hindering America's lasting economic recovery.

If there's one thing entrepreneurs hate most about government, it's unpredictability. The complaint about the current administration I hear more than any other from businesspeople is that they cannot invest with confidence because they have no idea what policies they will face. Not surprisingly, then, research has shown that policy uncertainty harms growth and has hampered our nation's economic recovery.[10] Economists from Stanford University and the University of Chicago have calculated that between 2006 and 2011, entrepreneurs' inability to predict government policy has lowered real GDP by about 1.4 percentage points per year and lowered employment by around 2.5 million jobs.[11]

Entrepreneurs say they are staying on the sidelines because they don't know what the future holds in three principle areas: ObamaCare's health reforms, the Dodd-Frank Act's financial market regulations, and proposed tax increases. Repeal of ObamaCare and Dodd-Frank would help economic growth dramatically, as would extending the so-called "Bush tax cuts" while starting real tax reform efforts.

Finally, if we want to spur growth, the U.S. must get serious about immigration policy. America needs more talented people to come to our shores. Right now, the debate about immigration is completely misdirected. Most pundits and politicians continue to focus on illegal immigration. Meanwhile, they are ignoring the most destructive immigration policy of all: expelling foreign students and professionals after their student and temporary visas expire. Recent research shows that for every immigrant with education in science, technology, mathematics, or engineering, 2.62 new jobs are created for native-born Americans.[12]

To grow the economy, the U.S. needs to increase productivity, and in order to increase productivity, it needs a skilled and entrepreneurial labor force. Every student with a clean legal record who obtains a degree from an American university should automatically have the right to become a permanent resident. People who worry that those students will create unemployment for Americans are misguided. Skilled and talented immigrants create jobs, opportunity, and growth; they do not take them away.

One moral point on this last issue is worth making. We shouldn't forget that for almost all of us, immigration is our own family story. If you are glad to be an American, thank the immigrants who risk it all to come to the U.S.

### ISSUE 2: PUTTING AMERICA BACK TO WORK

Making the moral case for job creation is not hard: Jobs are not just a source of money for Americans; they are a ticket to earned success. High unemployment, especially when it is avoidable, is fundamentally unfair because it robs people of their potential fulfillment. It is especially harmful to the poor and the young, who have had fewer economic opportunities than others. As of November 2011, unemployment for the sixteen-to-nineteen age group is running at 23.7 percent, close to the highest teenage unemployment rate on record.[13]

Unemployment is also getting in the way of life's greatest joys, such as marriage, starting a family, and pursuing education. When the young are hurt by persistent unemployment, they delay many of these decisions.

On the current policy path, America will face permanently higher levels of unemployment, just like its social democratic European allies. A return to free enterprise principles would allow

America's entrepreneurs to create private-sector jobs. The choice, for millions of fellow citizens, is between welfare checks and paychecks. That is the moral choice between earned success and learned helplessness.

Here are the depressing facts about unemployment in America today that show the urgency of making better policy:

- Unemployment rose from 4.7 percent in January 2006 to 7.8 percent when President Obama took office in January 2009.[14] By October 2009, unemployment reached to 10.1 percent, and hovered above 9 percent for a twenty-one-month stretch from May 2009 to January 2011—the longest such period since the Great Depression.[15] As of December 2011, the unemployment rate was still 8.5 percent.[16]

- Fourteen million is the official jobless number, but it isn't the one that matters. An additional 8.8 million people are involuntary part-time workers and another 2.6 million are "frustrated workers," having quit searching for a job even though they would work if they could.[17] Combined, these three groups total approximately 25.4 million people, or 16.5 percent of the labor force.

- A 2011 nationwide survey found that 18 percent of young people said they delayed marriage due to job worries or unemployment; 23 percent delayed starting a family; and 27 percent delayed furthering their educations.[18]

When talking about job creation, we need to stay focused on three core principles.

*First*, the government is terrible at "picking winners" in the economy. With the stimulus spending of the past several years the government has tried to dictate the parts of the economy that deserve public-sector support, and the parts that don't. These policies usually lead to failure and hurt job growth.

*Second*, the government must guard against special interests, including organized labor and the crony corporations with disproportionate access to government power. When special interests set policy or embed themselves in the government itself, job creation suffers.

*Finally*, the government needs to keep its payroll to a minimum. Obviously, there is a need for a staffed public sector, but government jobs are not a good substitute for private-sector jobs when it comes to reducing unemployment.

AT THE OUTSET of the current recession, the Obama administration's economists promised a swift decline in unemployment if only Americans would agree to large increases in the size and scope of government.[19] We got only half the deal, though: government exploded, while unemployment stayed high. The government economists are scratching their heads, but there really is no mystery here. Businesses are not hiring precisely because of public-sector growth, excessive regulation, labor market interference, and tax complexity.

First, consider the massive growth in government regulation in the past three years. As we saw a moment ago, the Dodd-Frank Act has produced regulatory costs and uncertainty that are actively dissuading businesses from expanding, which means they are not hiring.[20] The same is true of ObamaCare, which is discouraging firms from creating jobs because they do not know what the mandated cost of doing so will be in the coming years. Scrapping these programs is a primary job-growing priority, according to many economists.[21]

Government growth—even the creation of government jobs—also crowds out employment. This seems counterintuitive to a lot of people—a job created by government adds to total employment, right? Wrong. Economists have shown that the administration's stimulus spending created or saved 450,000 government jobs but destroyed or forestalled 1 million private-sector jobs.[22] We saw in Chapter 5 that every government job costs between 1 and 2.2 private-sector jobs. This is because of the detrimental tax and public debt effects on investment and confidence, as well as the fact that government tends to crowd out the more-productive private sector when engaged in the same basic activities.[23] Downsizing the federal workforce will increase net American employment.

Another way the government destroys jobs while claiming to create them is by subsidizing favored industries. Take, for instance, the administration's "green jobs" initiatives—to subsidize companies that develop sustainable energy and products. These initiatives actually *destroy* jobs by diverting profitable private investment into public subsidies to industries that are not financially viable. Consider the case of the solar company Solyndra, which received $535 million in federal government loan guarantees. The U.S. Energy Secretary called the guarantees "part of President Obama's aggressive strategy to put Americans back to work."[24] Solyndra estimated that the complex covered by the government's support would employ 3,000 people. Instead, Solyndra went belly-up in 2011 (meaning zero new jobs). There are dozens of Solyndra-like boondoggles that are not yet in the news. Government efforts such as this should be abandoned and replaced with a pledge to get rid of *all* subsidies.

Reasonable people disagree about whether labor unions are a good or bad thing for America, on balance. But almost everyone knows that they increase labor prices and thus drive down hiring.

One of the worst things the government can do in periods of high unemployment, therefore, is to push the private economy toward greater unionization. Unfortunately, that is exactly what has happened. The administration's $787 billion economic stimulus package in 2009 was preceded by an executive order from President Obama strongly encouraging—in effect mandating—that government agencies only use unionized firms for large-scale construction projects.[25]

The administration's pro-union policies don't stop with the economic stimulus. Consider the recent activities of the National Labor Relations Board (NLRB) toward the airplane manufacturer Boeing. The NLRB filed a complaint against the company, in an attempt to coerce Boeing to move airplane construction from non-union South Carolina to union-heavy Washington State.[26] While the case was litigated, four thousand workers in South Carolina sat idle during the worst period of unemployment in decades. (The case was dropped in December 2011, but not until Boeing agreed not to build another plant in South Carolina.[27]) This sort of labor interference cripples job creation by making companies more hesitant to invest in new plants, keeping labor sidelined, and lowering productivity.

Tax reform is also essential to job creation. A simpler, more efficient tax code would allocate resources more effectively and stimulate economic growth. It would reward the most productive firms, not the cleverest accountants and the companies most closely tied to politicians. And it would draw investment to the United States. Employment markets would improve as a result.

In sum, the government is impeding the ability of entrepreneurs to create jobs. The solution is *less government*, not more. One practical way to do this, especially in the case of regulation, might be to require that the government issue an Employment

Impact Statement for new policies before they are enacted. Few issues are more important to the American people than jobs—and the government should know exactly how many of them will be lost as a result of raising costs on employers.

## ISSUE 3: GETTING THE UNITED STATES OUT OF DEBT

Most people see private debt as a moral issue. We've all known people who live beyond their means and fail to pay back their debts. We judge them harshly for being irresponsible and self-centered.

If debt is a moral issue at an individual level, it can be a moral issue at the national level, too. The U.S. is the world's most successful nation. Yet years of profligate government spending and poor planning have left America in a huge debt crisis. Unless it reduces deficits and stabilizes its government spending relative to the size of the economy, it will have just three choices: steal from future generations, inflate the currency to lower the real value of the debt, or refuse to repay those to whom it owes money. All these options are immoral because they are unfair: They harm others who have done no harm to America.

Many European allies are in economic crisis and will face austerity for at least a decade. The reason is simple: They lived beyond their means for years by borrowing to pay for current consumption and government services. Today, the bills are due, and the rest of the world is increasingly unwilling to lend them money. Americans have to choose whether to accept that same future or not. What kind of country will we leave our children? One that offers the opportunity we have enjoyed—or one that leaves our kids to foot the bill for the current generation's inability to curb government spending? In my view, the moral answer is obvious.

Here are a few facts that show how urgent it is that America fix its debt problems:

- The CBO estimates that, at the end of fiscal 2011, the federal government's gross debt is 100 percent of annual GDP.[28] Economists find that countries rarely are able to recover from this crushing level of debt without falling into decline.[29] America is at the edge of an economic abyss.

- The U.S. government's deficit in 2010 alone was $1.3 trillion (8.9 percent of GDP), and the CBO estimates that the fiscal 2011 deficit will also reach this level.[30] To put this into perspective, in 2011, the U.S. will borrow about $4,152 for every person in America,[31] *to pay for a government that 65 percent of Americans already believe is too large.*[32]

- Servicing the national debt in 2011 cost an estimated $221 billion.[33] Debt service costs will reach $1 trillion in 2023 under current policies. Considering the level of debt, this is actually a bargain because of historically low interest rates. If the interest rates the U.S. pays on its debt were to rise by just one percentage point, it would cost an extra $1.7 trillion over the coming decade.[34]

- Under current policies, federal spending will exceed revenue by 10.1 percent of GDP over the next twenty-five years. Even ignoring the existing debt, closing that gap completely with taxes would require an immediate and permanent 56 percent increase in all federal tax revenues.[35]

There are three core principles to keep in mind when addressing the debt crisis.

*First,* the debt problem has one fundamental cause that outweighs all others: out-of-control entitlement spending. The U.S.

cannot fix the deficit and debt problems without taking on entitlement reform. Any politician who suggests otherwise is not telling the truth.

*Second*, debt crises are more successfully dealt with through spending reductions than with tax increases. This is just common sense. If you took over a private company that was failing because of out-of-control spending, you would focus first on spending, not raising prices. Only governments have the nerve to argue that profligate spending can be fixed with more confiscatory taxation.

*Third*, there are no quick fixes. The national debt is a vast and long-term problem. The scope of a consolidation plan must reflect this reality. Any proposal that does not deal with the long run— at least twenty-five years—is not serious.

AMERICA IS NOT the first country to face a debt problem. Many other nations have faced such problems. Some have returned to solid footing and prosperity. Others have failed, leading either to default or years of malaise. We can learn a lot from the paths other countries have taken.

A group of American Enterprise Institute (AEI) economists recently looked closely at twenty-one developed countries' attempts to reduce debt and deficits (economists call this "fiscal consolidation") from 1970 to 2007.[36] Like America today, all these countries had spent too much money for too long. In response, some countries cut spending radically, while others tried to get more tax money from their citizens. Still others tried a combination of spending cuts and tax increases.

Some of the countries succeeded and escaped their crises. Others defaulted on their debts or limped along in long-term economic recession. Of the nations that succeeded, 85 percent of their deficit reduction, on average, came from spending cuts. Of those that failed, spending cuts were only 47 percent. In a nutshell, cutters succeeded, and taxers failed.

Again, all this may seem like common sense. Countries that meet spending problems head on with spending cuts inspire confidence among investors. Those that meet their overspending with tax increases are treated in much the same way as financially irresponsible individuals—no one wants to lend to them or go into business with them. But that common sense is often sadly lacking among politicians who have the ability to collect tax money by force.

What sort of spending did the successful countries cut? You guessed it: entitlements. Reducing entitlements is the single most effective step a country can take toward reducing its national debt. The reason is simple: Entitlement programs become more expensive over time. Every dollar of savings from reducing entitlement spending today is accompanied by many more dollars of savings in the future. The lesson for America is that changes to Medicare or Social Security right now will pay big dividends into the future.[37]

But all the benefits of entitlement reform are not far off in the future—some come right now. Economists at the International Monetary Fund have shown that cutting entitlements can have an immediate, positive impact on the current economy.[38] The reason is that when global investors see a country deal with its long-term spending problems, it bolsters confidence and attracts capital, growth, and jobs. If America deals with entitlements now, foreigners will be more likely to invest their money and establish their businesses in the U.S. That is precisely what the nation needs to emerge from the economic slump.

The bottom line when it comes to debt and deficits is this: If the U.S. can get entitlements under control, it can achieve budget balance. For years, irresponsible politicians from both parties have

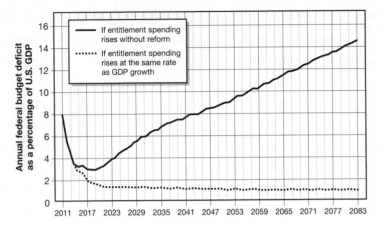

***Figure 7.2.*** *Entitlement spending is the real cause of the U.S. govern-ment debt explosion. (Source: Author's calculations. Congressional Budget Office Long-Term Budget Outlook, June 2011, Alternative Fiscal Scenario.)*

made promises to the American people about their pensions and their health care—promises that simply cannot be fulfilled. If the U.S. does not deal with entitlement reform, particularly of Social Security and Medicare, debt will continue to explode, and future generations will pay the price.

While entitlements are the main problem leading to debt and deficits, discretionary spending—the spending that the government approves every year—can and should be cut as well. Many good proposals have shown how this can be done. President Obama's Fiscal Commission in 2010—which to date he has ignored—recommended cutting $84 billion from discretionary spending in 2012, $153 billion in 2013, and a total of almost $2 trillion between 2012 and 2020.[39]

A number of discretionary programs should be slashed right away. Prime among them are agricultural subsidies, which cost the nation nearly $20 billion each year,[40] drive up food prices, and hurt farmers in poor countries around the world. Similarly, the U.S. subsidizes both fossil fuel and "clean energy," distorting markets and putting almost $20 billion in tax money into corporate pockets each year.[41] Examples like this are, sadly, easy to find.

America can also save money by reducing the federal workforce. The government could cut 10 percent of federal workers— 200,000 jobs–relatively painlessly by not replacing those who retire or quit. This would save taxpayers $13.2 billion by 2015.[42] In addition to cutting jobs, a three-year compensation freeze (in wages or benefits) could be imposed on federal workers and Defense Department civilians, which would save $20.4 billion by 2015.[43]

Cutting spending on entitlements, discretionary spending, and the federal workforce would go a long way toward reducing the national debt. But shouldn't we also raise taxes to close the gap?

No. In fact, the government should match spending cuts with tax *de*creases, especially on businesses. Taxing companies at very high rates leads some to pay more, but others to lower their production or go overseas. As a result, they pay less in taxes. As I will show, the U.S. could lower corporate taxes and raise *more* money for the Treasury than it does currently.

ISSUE 4: FIXING ENTITLEMENTS

As any child knows, it is wrong to make promises you cannot keep—and even worse to make promises you have no intention of keeping. That is the essential moral problem with our creaking system of entitlements.

The promises politicians have made to their constituents have created massive unfunded liabilities in pensions and health care. These programs have made millions of Americans dependent on the government, which has promised them more in benefits than they ever paid into the system.

Without immediate reform, the insolvent system will require that future generations pay in much more than they take out, which is manifestly unfair. If people are unable or unwilling to pay for future benefits and the system goes bankrupt, those most harmed will be the poor, who will lose their safety net. A system that allows people a free ride at the expense of the least powerful members of society—the young and the poor—is blatantly unethical.

Here are the facts about the entitlement system that show the urgent need for reform:

- To date, most Americans have withdrawn more from the Social Security and Medicare systems than they ever paid into them.[44] In the coming decades, most people will have to pay in more than they take out, costing tens of trillions of dollars.

- Social Security and Medicare are going broke because benefit payments are exceeding the taxes to pay for them. The fund to pay for Medicare hospital care has been running a deficit since 2008.[45] Without reform, Social Security will be insolvent in 2036.[46]

- The U.S. currently spends 9.9 percent of GDP on entitlements ($1.49 trillion). Without reform, by 2030, that number will rise to 14.3 percent ($3.43 billion).[47]

- Despite the appalling costs, the system fails many of the neediest citizens. The U.S. currently spends over $725 billion per year on Social Security benefits, yet leaves almost 10 percent of seniors in poverty.[48]

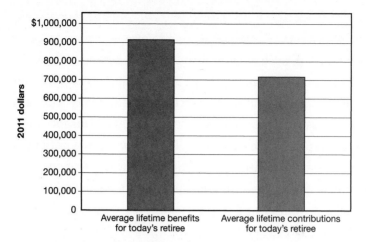

***Figure 7.3.*** *Americans retiring today are going to take out more than they have paid in to Medicare and Social Security. (Source: Urban Institute. Steuerle, C. Eugene, and Rennane, Stephanie. "Social Security and Medicare Taxes and Benefits Over a Lifetime," Urban Institute, June 2011.)*

Before I discuss the specific policies needed to enact reform, there are three fundamental principles underlying a fair and stable entitlements system.

*First*, entitlements should be a minimum basic safety net for the poor, not a source of retirement benefits for everybody. The government should move away from a system that is effectively for the middle class.

*Second*, entitlement policy should not create incentives for people to stop working and saving their money. The system should encourage people to work longer, retire later, and save more, so they can take care of themselves without resorting to the safety net.

*Third*, the system must create incentives for people to use public resources in a responsible way. Entitlements should not reward governments or individuals for overspending on programs and services, as they currently do.

• • •

BASED ON THESE PRINCIPLES, we can reform entitlements, and in the process, solve much of our problem with debt.

Let's start with Social Security. The system is going broke, and many politicians would have us believe that the only way to fix this is by raising taxes. The easiest way to do so, they say, is by lifting the cap on taxable earnings. Right now, people pay payroll taxes on their first $106,800 of earnings for Social Security. If people paid payroll taxes on all their income, it would create a flood of new money and a huge tax increase on upper-income Americans.[49]

This is nothing more than a sneaky way to make our tax system more progressive, and it is completely unnecessary. There is no reason to do this. The system can be fixed without more taxes, in three steps.

*First*, the retirement age is absurdly low. Unless you are in a heavy physical industry or have a health issue, why should you retire at 65? You'll still be in your prime. The U.S. should gradually raise the retirement age to age seventy by 2065, indexed to longevity (meaning that the retirement age will continue to increase as people live longer, which no doubt they will).

Believe it or not, the retirement age for receiving benefits has only increased by one year (from 65 to 66) since the system was founded in 1935. In 1935, the average man living at age 65 would survive an additional 12.7 years, and the average woman, an additional 14.7 years.[50] Now those numbers are 18.7 and 20.8 years, respectively. In addition, more people retire early today than they did when Social Security started. It is not hard to see why the system is unsustainable.[51] People live longer and better lives today and can work productively for more years. Social Security should reflect this fact.

*Second*, index benefits to price inflation because that is what matters when it comes to maintaining seniors' standard of living. The government currently raises benefits on the basis of wage inflation, which is higher than price inflation. This doesn't make sense, because Social Security is intended as a way to support the elderly, not as a salary reflecting the increasing productivity of current workers. By making this small change, the U.S. would save $7.6 trillion over seventy-five years.[52]

*Third*, gradually adopt means testing and reduce benefits for earners whose incomes are so high that Social Security is not a major part of their retirement income. This recognizes that the safety net is not intended to provide benefits to people who are not in poverty and moves America away from a system in which middle- and upper-class people become dependent on the government for retirement income they could and should generate on their own. A few nondraconian changes (lowering spousal benefits slightly and reducing the percentages of wages that Social Security replaces for high earners, for example) would save about $3.2 trillion over seventy-five years.[53]

Together, these reforms would keep the current Social Security system solvent in perpetuity without raising the cap on contributions or raising the payroll tax rate.

If making major changes, however, why not build a whole new system? Imagine a system that is cheaper than the current one, is not in danger of insolvency, better protects seniors, and is not a kind of welfare for the middle class.[54] What would that look like?

To begin with, as with the reforms I have already described, the U.S. would need to raise retirement ages to reflect the happy reality that people are living longer, healthier lives. People should be given a positive incentive to work longer through the elimination of the Social Security payroll taxes for individuals aged sixty-two and over and of the "Social Security Retirement Earnings Test," which lowers Social Security benefits to workers if they earn money.

In addition, we should give people ownership over their retirement savings, instead of putting them into the government "trust funds" that are systematically raided by politicians. All workers age 55 and younger should be enrolled in an actual retirement savings account funded by 5 percent of a worker's earnings (2.5 percent from the individual and a matching 2.5 percent from the employer). This would be like a universal IRA account and would supplement workers' own voluntary retirement savings. It would be owned and controlled by the individual.

Next, all seniors should be guaranteed a standard of living above poverty. It is shocking to think that, with all the U.S. currently spends, it still hasn't managed to care adequately for all senior citizens.[55] A basic income supplement could provide enough income to bring all low-income seniors to above the level of poverty (provided they use it wisely), paid for with a tax on wages well below 6 percent. This would be an actual safety net and would cost about 60 percent of what the U.S. currently pays for Social Security.[56]

These simple reforms would achieve the four things America needs from the Social Security system: solvency, keeping the elderly out of poverty, ensuring that people save something for their retirement, and giving citizens—not politicians—control over retirement savings. And by keeping costs manageable, the reforms will ensure that Social Security is around for future generations.

SOCIAL SECURITY is only one of the bloated entitlement programs that threaten America's future. Medicare (providing health care for seniors) and Medicaid (providing health care for the poor) are arguably much bigger problems. Medicare in particular has been expanding faster than any other area of government, growing by 180 percent in real dollars from 1990 to 2010.[57]

Medicare and Medicaid are out of control not just because of high inflation in health costs but because the government has made open-ended commitments to citizens, regardless of cost. Imagine trying to operate a supermarket where "members" pay a low monthly fee and are then invited to take anything they "need" off the shelf. That's more or less the Medicare and Medicaid model.

Let's start with Medicaid, which is intended to give the poor medical coverage. The states administer Medicaid, with a subsidy from Washington. The federal government currently matches state dollars spent on the program, at a rate of between one-to-one and three-to-one (depending on the state). So if Arizona, which receives a 2.06:1 match, spends $1,000 treating a poor person, it gets $2,060 from the federal government. There is no limit on federal support—the more Arizona spends, the more the federal government spends. Arizona (and every other state) has the incentive to expand Medicaid programs wastefully, because the federal government is picking up the tab. Every dollar Arizona spends means $3.06 in total health care expenditures.[58]

Not surprisingly, states are offering Medicaid services to more and more people—and not just poor people. Take the case of New York. While that state's poverty rate is 14.2 percent, 27 percent of New Yorkers in 2009 got their health care through Medicaid, costing federal taxpayers $29.3 billion.[59] Simply put, the federal government makes it too economical for New York—a traditionally liberal state prone to extravagant government spending on social services—to offer Medicaid to too many people who are not poor.

There is a relatively straightforward solution to this problem: Provide the federal subsidy as block grants to the states—that is, send the states checks for the year's total federal allotment—and let them use it as they see fit. If New York wants to be profligate and overspend, it can do it with its own money, not with unlimited federal tax dollars coming from places like Kentucky and Texas. States would have the incentive to economize and innovate within a fixed budget, just as private companies (and all individuals) do.

While excessive expenditure on Medicaid poses a major budget problem for America, Medicare is even worse. The program guarantees *unlimited* payment for the health-care costs for the rapidly growing population of seniors. The CBO projects that Medicare spending will grow from $521 billion in 2011 to $725 billion in real (inflation-adjusted) dollars in 2020, a growth rate 3.3 percentage points higher than inflation.[60] If no changes are made to the current law, Medicare spending will be gobbling up 5.9 percent of American GDP by 2035.[61]

Runaway Medicare spending occurs because the system treats seniors the same way the Medicaid system treats states; it takes away any incentive for people to live within a budget. Predictably, nobody does. Without reform, Medicare will almost singlehandedly bankrupt the country.

To fix the system, two things are needed: Keep people in the workforce (and on private insurance, if possible), and move away from guaranteeing unlimited health benefits without regard to cost.

First, the U.S. should gradually raise the age for receiving Medicare benefits to sixty-seven. This is a minor change that no reasonable person can deny makes sense, looking at the improved health of seniors in the past decades. Government disability benefits will still be available to those who need them. Also, the Medicare payroll taxes for individuals aged sixty-two and older should be eliminated so there are better incentives for older Americans to work.

Second, the U.S. must move away from "defined benefits" (where the government guarantees unlimited services) to "defined contributions" (where the government guarantees a certain level of insurance coverage). Your employer most likely provides health benefits to you. That means they guarantee they will make insurance payments on your behalf (which are defined contributions), not pay all your medical bills (which would be defined benefits). The government needs to use this kind of model as well. There is no other way to contain costs.

Each senior citizen should be guaranteed a fixed payment adjusted for age, income, and health status. This payment would go into an individual account, from which seniors would pay for health insurance provided by private companies that guaranteed certain minimum coverage levels. Seniors who wanted generous "Cadillac" health care plans could have them, provided they were willing to pay the difference out of their own pockets. Those who chose more cost-efficient plans would get to keep the savings. This would cap the government's exposure and encourage seniors to make cost-effective insurance decisions according to their desires and needs. The Federal Employees Health Benefits Program works this way, so it would not be a radical departure from government procedures.[62]

To reiterate the central point: If politicians do just one thing to help get America's fiscal house in order, it should be entitlement reform. And if there is just one entitlement reform, it should be Medicare. Without this single reform, nothing else will solve our debt and deficit problem.

ISSUE 5: REFORMING THE TAX CODE

Some believe that taxation is a dry topic with no moral significance, but nothing could be further from the truth.

The current tax system is hobbling American free enterprise. It penalizes earned success by taxing productive activity at rates that are internationally uncompetitive. It unfairly picks winners and losers in the economy with thousands upon thousands of special deals and loopholes for well-connected companies and individuals. It weakens American citizenship by exempting half the working population from paying any federal income taxes.

The status quo system is confiscatory, unfair, needlessly complex, and at odds with all of the elements of a moral system. Major tax reform should be a top priority for reasons that extend well beyond simple economic efficiency.

We have already looked at a number of the disheartening facts about our tax system, but here are the key ones to remember in any debate:

- Although two-thirds of Americans believe that everyone should be required to pay some amount to fund the government, in 2011, 46 percent of households had zero or negative federal income tax liability.[63] Even when payroll taxes are added in, 28 percent of households had zero or negative federal tax liability.[64]

- In 2010, before any of President Obama's policies were implemented, 60 percent of families received more from the government than they paid in taxes. That number is inching toward 70 percent, as the president pushes through various pieces of his agenda.[65]

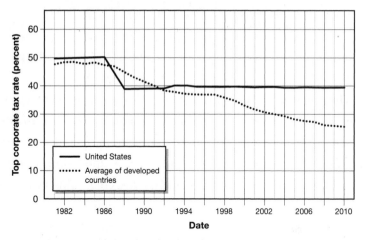

***Figure 7.4.*** *While other developed countries have lowered their corporate tax rates, the U.S. rate remains uncompetitively high. (Source: OECD Tax Database. Available at www.oecd.org/ctp /taxdatabase. Note: The rates shown are the top statutory combined corporate tax rates. The average of developed countries represents the OECD average.)*

- The complexity of the system has significant costs. Americans spend 6.1 billion hours a year in preparing their personal taxes.[66] The cost of complying with the individual and corporate income taxes in 2008 amounted to $163 billion, or more than $500 per person.[67]

- The U.S. top combined corporate tax rate, which includes both federal and (average) state taxes, is 39.2 percent, the second highest in the industrialized world.[68]

In thinking about how to reform the tax system, there are four principles to keep in mind.

*First*, taxes should never be used to pursue social engineering objectives. The point of taxes is to raise the revenues necessary to operate the government America wants, not to reward the politically well connected or increase income equality.

*Second*, taxes should distort productive activity as little as possible. That means lowering marginal tax rates and closing tax loopholes for special interests—even if they are good for us or our friends.

*Third*, the tax system should not harm citizenship by making government effectively free for a large part of the population. In addition to closing loopholes, the base of people who pay income taxes should be broadened. Everyone should pay something, even a small amount, so they remember that the government is not free.

*Fourth*, a major factor in the current economic crisis is that Americans tend to consume too much and save too little. The tax system should not penalize savings and investment.


AMERICA IS HORRIBLY IN DEBT, as we have seen over and over again in this book. All "fairness" arguments aside, many sensible people believe that tax rates need to rise because the government simply needs more money. But readers can reject that argument for two reasons: (1) the country has a spending problem, not a revenue problem; and (2) it is demonstrably wrong that raising income tax rates will necessarily raise government revenues.

A simple tax principle is that if the income tax rate is zero, income tax revenues will be zero. If income tax rates are 100 percent, income tax revenues will still be zero. Why? Because with a 100 percent tax rate, nobody will bother to work and companies will not produce—at least, not officially. Somewhere between zero percent and 100 percent lies the tax rate that brings in the most tax revenue. This idea is often referred to as the "Laffer Curve," named after Reagan administration economist Arthur Laffer.[69] Laffer noted that if taxes were high enough, we could lower rates and get *more* tax revenues, because people would work more, invest more, and produce more.

Where is the U.S. on the Laffer Curve today? If the U.S. raises taxes, will it drive revenues up, or down? For corporate taxes, the evidence suggests the latter: there would be *more* revenue with *lower* rates. AEI economists have estimated that if the corporate tax rate were lowered from 35 percent to 26.4 percent, the expanded production and investment by firms would bring in $748 billion in extra revenues over the next ten years. Obviously, this would also mean faster growth and lower unemployment.[70]

Defending high corporate taxes is easy for politicians. All they have to say is that corporations are not people and that they make a lot of money. They forget that all corporate income ultimately goes to people, so corporate taxes are a double taxation on personal incomes. Whose incomes? "Millionaires and billionaires," as the president often refers to them.

Actually, it's not the millionaires and billionaires who pay most corporate taxes. If you want to see who really pays, look in the mirror. Corporate taxes are expenses for firms. When they go up, firms cut back on production and other expenditures. This means less demand for labor, and downward pressure on wages. In other words, corporate taxes are—at least partly—passed on to workers in the form of lower pay. Economists find that up to 75 percent of the real burden of the corporate income tax falls on workers, not capital owners.[71] The primary beneficiaries of a decrease in the corporate tax rate would be wage earners, not "corporate fat cats."

Lowering personal income taxes is important as well, because it will induce people to work and invest more than they otherwise would, resulting in higher growth.[72] Economists estimate that a top marginal personal income tax rate of 20 percent (compared to 35 percent today, and 39.6 percent, proposed by President Obama) would maximize long-run economic growth.[73] An even more direct way to increase savings and investment is to lower taxes on capital gains, interest, and dividends.

THE U.S. TAX CODE is 16,845 pages long.[74] Why, you ask? The answer is that it is a rather *detailed* document. There is, for example, a special provision for the favorable tax treatment of racehorses. And not just any racehorses—only those two years old or younger. Section 68(e)(3)(a)(i)(I) creates a special investment depreciation schedule for those fine creatures.[75] Somebody with an interest in young racehorses most likely got a politician to write this provision into the tax code and probably saved a bundle on his taxes in the process.

This is called a "tax loophole," or what economists euphemistically call a "tax expenditure." The tax code is a Swiss cheese of these details. The racehorse loophole may cost the Treasury and taxpayers only a little; others cost a lot more. These loopholes have to be eliminated to make the tax system fairer and less distorted.

That's easier said than done, of course. You may not benefit from the racehorse loophole, but you probably do benefit from others. For example, the top two personal income tax loopholes are the exclusion of employer contributions for health premiums, and the deduction for mortgage interest on homes. In the first case, you don't have to pay taxes on your health-care premiums. That can easily save you $1,000 a year or more. In the second instance, you don't have to pay taxes on the money you spend on mortgage interest, which can easily save you several thousand dollars (if you own your house). These two policies alone make up 35 percent of all taxes lost to loopholes. Without them, government revenue would increase by approximately $1.1 trillion over five years.[76]

These two loopholes will be difficult to reform, to be sure. But Americans need to realize that both are hurting the country in a way that goes far beyond money. One distorts health markets by making insurance a non-taxable benefit and thus look cheaper than it really is. The other helped create the conditions for the housing crisis by subsidizing home ownership. If you dislike the mess the housing and health-care systems are in, in part you can blame these tax loopholes.

Corporate loopholes are no better. The top five make up 55 percent of all corporate tax expenditures and will cost the economy about $218 billion over the next five years.[77] Getting rid of these programs would make the economy both fairer and more efficient.

Without loopholes, won't taxes automatically rise? Not necessarily. The tax rates could be lowered by an amount that offsets the value of loopholes, so money isn't taken from taxpayers to fuel government expansion.

THE REFORMS I'VE PROPOSED are based on the assumption that the current tax code is worth saving and fixing. But what if we could replace the whole system? What if we pulled the system up by its roots and replaced it with one that is simpler, better, and less corruptible? What would such a system look like?

Many reformers favor a flat tax with no deductions. Slightly more complicated but better, in the view of some economists, would be a move to a true consumption tax. That means people would pay taxes on what they spend to consume, not on what they save or invest. Estimates by the Treasury Department suggest that a switch from the current system to a consumption tax (with rates similar to the current income tax) would add about 4.5 percent to the national income over the next twenty years (about $657 billion).[78]

In sum, there are huge opportunities to improve our tax system from the current monstrosity to one that better matches our values and needs.

AS I STATED AT THE OUTSET, my goal in this chapter was not to provide a full policy platform, but to demonstrate the right way to set up arguments for policy reform, using today's key policy dilemmas as case studies. Every section could be expanded into full studies, and for that reason the website for this book (www.aei.org.arthurbrooks) contains expanded references and further reading sources on each policy area.

There are many facts and figures in the previous sections because free enterprise must make sense empirically if it is to make sense at all—and we can be confident that it does. But let's not forget the main point of this book: that free enterprise is a matter of the heart even more than the head. Whether we're discussing taxation or Medicare, deficits or jobs, public policy should first and foremost be an expression of values. As free enterprise advocates, we can take comfort in knowing the facts and data are on our side, but we must first show that the moral arguments are on our side as well if we want to prevail.

# The Road to Freedom

Our country faces a lot of choices today.

We are deciding between monetary policies, tax systems, and political parties. These things are important and we need to get them right. But the most important choice we face is deeper than any individual policy or election. It is a choice between two ideas of America.

The first idea is that the key to our success as a nation resides with the government. Practically, the government will restart our economy with more stimulus, more taxes, and more borrowing. Morally, the government holds the secret to fairness through more income redistribution and taxation of the wealthy. The government will lift up the poor and disadvantaged. We need government programs in order to pursue our happiness.

The second idea of America is that the key to our success lies in free enterprise—the system our Founders left us to maximize liberty, create individual opportunity, and reward entrepreneurship. Free enterprise creates the opportunities our ancestors came to America seeking—the opportunities that allowed them to pursue their happiness in a new land. It is the free enterprise system that treated them fairly for the first time; instead of being penalized for lacking a noble birth, they were rewarded for their hard work and personal responsibility. Free enterprise made a country of immigrants into the most powerful, prosperous nation in the history of the world.

This second idea is not antigovernment. It does not hold that government employees are bad, that we all should make our own rules, or that we should dismantle the state. The entrepreneurial idea for America simply limits the government to its proper role. The government offers one tool to help provide a minimum basic safety net and solve some of the market failures that act as a barrier to private enterprise. Good government is only large enough to do these things.

The choice between these two very different ideas of America has dramatic consequences for our future: Will we see growing bureaucracy or more entrepreneurship? Will we be a culture of redistribution or a culture of aspiration? Will we be a nation of takers or a nation of makers?

Politicians who pretend that we do not have to choose between these two ideas of America are mistaken or less than honest. They want us to think that statism and free enterprise are ultimately compatible; that bureaucracy is not antagonistic to self-government; that we can remain exceptional when our system is indistinguishable from collectivist systems around the world. But this is deceit. Not choosing is effectively just the choice for big government. Unless we actively choose free enterprise and make the tough choices to limit the government, we will slip down the road toward European-style social democracy. We know this to be true because it has been happening for nearly a century.

To be honest, big government is an easier choice than free enterprise. In the short run, it allows us to avoid sacrifice. Politicians who ask for sacrifice face a tough battle with voters, so they tend not to. But this laziness—on our part and on the part of the governing class—endangers all of us in the long run. It will mean the end of our Founders' vision for our country. It will end any hope of limited government. And it will saddle our children and grandchildren with crushing debt.

Free enterprise can seem like an especially tough choice at the present moment for America. It requires us to make hard decisions about spending and borrowing, just as we struggle to end the Great Recession. It means doing without some things and saying no to powerful claimants, cronies, and sometimes even our friends.

But as I hope this book has shown, the rewards of free enterprise dramatically outweigh any costs. Free enterprise teaches us to earn success, not learn helplessness. It rewards merit, which is the fair thing to do. And in the end, it is the *only* system that can improve the lives of literally billions of poor people—here and around the world.

These are the reasons I believe free enterprise is the only moral choice for America.

# ACKNOWLEDGMENTS

MANY PEOPLE made this book a reality, and I'm grateful to a lot of people for their help. To begin with, my executive assistant Michael Threadgould kept me organized and on track throughout the project. And the book would have been impossible without excellent research assistance from Chad Hill and Lori Sanders.

While all errors are my own, expertise and generous advice on this project came from AEI's great scholars and staff, including Joe Antos, Rachel Ayerst Manfredi, Jason Bertsch, Andrew Biggs, Karlyn Bowman, Alex Brill, Josh Burek, Kayla Cook, Robin Currie, John Cusey, David Gerson, Ken Green, Kevin Hassett, Steven Hayward, David Holtkamp, John Makin, Matthew McKillip, Thomas Miller, Sophie Oreck, Veronika Polakova, Daniel Rothschild, Toby Stock, and Alan Viard. Special thanks go to Charles Murray and Nick Eberstadt, AEI scholars whose work has deeply influenced mine and who carefully read drafts of this book. Likewise, AEI trustees Tully Friedman and Frank Hanna gave me invaluable advice all along the way.

Beyond AEI, I would like to express gratitude to a number of key individuals who gave me suggestions or material for this book. In particular, I would like to thank Christopher Chandler, Bernie

Marcus, Chuck Schwab, John Mackey, Mark Stoleson, Alan McCormick, Kevin Lewis, Ed Crane, Pete Wehner, and Jon Haidt, as well as my friends at AEI's sister organizations and in the media who provided important feedback on early versions of the manuscript.

I would like to thank my editor Lara Heimert at Basic Books, and my literary agent, Lisa Adams, at the Garamond Agency. Several of the key ideas here were developed in articles published on the editorial pages of the *Wall Street Journal* and the *Washington Post*, for which I am grateful to Paul Gigot, Howard Dickman, Rob Pollock, and Carlos Lozada.

I am humbled by the trust and support of the outstanding members—past and present—of AEI's Board of Trustees and National Council. For support on this project, all of us at AEI would especially like to thank the Anschutz Foundation, the Douglas and Maria DeVos Foundation, the Kern Family Foundation, the Charles Koch Foundation, Legatum, the Marcus Foundation, Jack and Pina Templeton, and the Triad Foundation.

As always, I am particularly indebted to my intellectual partner (and wife), Ester Munt-Brooks, who—as an American by choice instead of by birth—constantly reminded me why our free enterprise system is a moral one at its core. And thanks to our three children Joaquim, Carlos, and Marina, who endured being told many times to leave Dad alone because he is working on his book.

All royalties from this book go to support the work of the American Enterprise Institute.

# NOTES

CHAPTER ONE

1 Lydia Saad, "Americans Express Historic Negativity Toward U.S. Government," Gallup.com, September 26, 2011, http://www.gallup.com/poll/149678 /Americans-Express-Historic-Negativity-Toward-Government.aspx?utm _source=tagrss&utm_medium=rss&utm_campaign=syndication.

2 Polling data show, for example, that when asked what effect they expect from the health care bill, more Americans say they expect it to increase health-care costs than say they expect it to decrease costs, and more Americans expect the health-care bill to make health care worse than expect it to make care better. See Jeffery M. Jones, "Many Americans Doubt Costs, Benefits of Healthcare Reform," Gallup.com, September 16, 2009. www.gallup.com/ poll/122969/many-americans-doubt-costs-benefits-heatlthcare-reform.aspx

3 The current debt estimate comes from http://www.brillig.com/debt_clock/.

4 Frank Newport, "Despite Negativity, Americans Mixed on Ideal Role of Gov't," Gallup.com, September 28, 2011, http://www.gallup.com/poll/149741 /Despite-Negativity-Americans-Mixed-Ideal-Role-Gov.aspx.

5 Bret Stephens, "Lessons From Europe (Take 2)," *Wall Street Journal*, August 16, 2011, http://online.wsj.com/article/SB100014240531119034809 04576510200756243420.html?mod=WSJ_Opinion_LEADTop.

6 Debt statistic from Organisation for Economic Co-operation and Development (2011), OECD.Stat, (database), doi: 10.1787/data-00285-en.

7 See Michael Novak, *The Spirit of Democratic Capitalism* (Madison Books, 1991); and Charles Murray, "The Happiness of the People," Irving Kristol Lecture, American Enterprise Institute, 2009.

8 Arthur Brooks, *The Battle: How the Fight Between Free Enterprise and Big Government Will Shape America's Future* (Basic Books, 2010).

9 Joel Roberts, "Poll: The Politics of Healthcare," CBS News/*New York Times*, June 14, 2010, http://www.cbsnews.com/stories/2007/03/01/opinion/polls /main2528357.shtml. According to a 2011 CBS news poll 51 percent of

Americans said that they disapproved of the healthcare law, versus 35 percent who approved of it. See http://www.american.com/archive /datapoint-entries/healthcare-update.

10 Jonathan Haidt, "The New Synthesis in Moral Psychology," *Science* 316, no. 5827 (May 18, 2007): 998–1002.

11 George Lakoff, *Don't Think of an Elephant!* (Chelsea Green Publishing, 2004). Another reason why statists win the moral debates about our system is that they have figured out better than the right how to "frame" the arguments. The master of political argument framing is George Lakoff, a linguist at the University of California, Berkeley. In his 2004 bestseller *Don't Think of an Elephant!*, Lakoff argues that when it comes to successful politics, those who control the moral language get to frame the debate and win the hearts of voters. In progressive framing, free enterprise advocates are rigid and selfish, and their inability to make a strong moral case for freedom has only reinforced this view.

12 Declaration of Independence, July 4, 1776.

13 Virginia Declaration of Rights, June 12, 1776.

14 Philip S. Foner, ed., "Thomas Jefferson to Henry Lee, May 8, 1825," *The Basic Writings of Thomas Jefferson* (Halcyon House, 1950), 802.

15 Yasmine Ryan, "How Tunisia's Revolution Began," Al Jazeera, January 26, 2011, http://english.aljazeera.net/indepth/features/2011/01/20111261218159 85483.html; Yasmine Ryan, "The Tragic Life of a Street Vendor," Al Jazeera, January 20, 2011, http://english.aljazeera.net/indepth /features/2011/01 /201111684242518839.html.

16 Leon Aron, "Everything You Think You Know About the Collapse of the Soviet Union Is Wrong," *Foreign Policy*, July-August 2011, http://www .foreignpolicy.com/articles/2011/06/20/everything_you_think_you_know _about_the_collapse_of_the_soviet_union_is_wrong

17 Ronald Reagan, State of the Union Address, January 27, 1987, http://www .presidency.ucsb.edu/ws/index.php?pid=34430#axzz1RL21sVlN

18 Charles A. Murray, *Losing Ground: American social policy, 1950–1980* (Basic Books, 1984).

19 Thomas Jefferson, *Notes on the State of Virginia*, ed. Frank Shuffelton (Penguin Books, 1999).

20 Franklin D. Roosevelt, "Annual Message to Congress," January 4, 1935, *The Public Papers and Addresses of Franklin D. Roosevelt, vol. 4, The Court Disapproves, 1935*, ed. Samuel Rosenman (Random House, 1938).

21 Murray, *Losing Ground*.

22 The legislation to reform welfare was the Personal Responsibility and Work Opportunity Reconciliation Act of 1996 (PRWORA).

23 U.S. Bureau of the Census, "Poverty in the United States: 1999"; "Income, Poverty, and Health Insurance Coverage: 2003"; http://www.whitehouse.gov /infocus/welfarereform; John J. DiIulio Jr., "Older & Wiser?" *The Weekly Standard* 011, no. 1 (2005).

24 John Ifcher, "The Happiness of Single Mothers after Welfare Reform," *The B.E. Journal of Economic Analysis & Policy* 11, no. 1 (2011): 4–22.

## CHAPTER TWO

1 Catherine Rampell, "The Self-Employed Are the Happiest," New York Times Economix Blog, September 16, 2009, http://economix.blogs.nytimes.com /2009/09/16/the-self-employed-are-the-happiest/

2 For salary information, see http://www.cbsalary.com/national-salary-chart .aspx?specialty=Small+Business+Owner&cty=&sid=&kw=Small +Business+Owner&jn=jn037&edu=&tid=105988; http://www.cbsalary.com /national-salary-chart.aspx?specialty=Small+Business+Owner&cty =&sid=&kw=Small+Business+Owner&jn=jn037&edu=&tid=105988. On the benefit differential between public and private workers, see Andrew Biggs and Jason Richwine, "Comparing Federal and Private Sector Compensation," American Enterprise Institute, Economic Policy Working Paper 2011-02, http://www.aei.org/docLib/AEI-Working-Paper-on-Federal-Pay-May-2011 .pdf

3 Lymari Morales, "Self-employed Workers Clock the Most Hours Each Week," Gallup.com, August 26, 2009, http://www.gallup.com/poll/122510 /Self-Employed-Workers-Clock-Hours-Week.aspx

4 Richard A. Easterlin, "Does Economic Growth Improve the Human Lot? Some Empirical Evidence," in *Nations and households in economic growth: Essays in honor of Moses Abramovitz*, eds. Paul A. David and Melvin W. Reder (Academic Press Inc, 1974), 89–125

5 More recently, economists Betsey Stevenson and Justin Wolfers have questioned the Easterlin Paradox, citing Gallup public opinion surveys from around the world. They conclude that rising national income levels do indeed raise national levels of subjective well-being. See Betsey Stevenson and Justin Wolfers, "Economic Growth and Subjective Well-Being: Reassessing the Easterlin Paradox," National Bureau of Economic Research, Working Paper No. 14282, August 2008, http://www.nber.org/papers/w14282.pdf. Economists over the decades have found other ways to examine the relationship between income and happiness. In a recent study, Nobel laureate Daniel Kahneman and his Princeton University colleague Angus Deaton analyzed a survey of 450,000 Americans in 2008 and 2009. The survey asked respondents to not only evaluate the quality of their lives, but also to report on their moods and levels of stress. They found that people who reported they were poor said that earning more money raised their mood, lowered their likelihood of depression, decreased stress, and made them more likely to evaluate the overall quality of their lives as higher. But this effect evaporated at about $75,000 per year in annual income. After that, people continued to *say* their life was getting better, but they actually got no happier: Their mood was not significantly brighter, they were no less susceptible to depression, and they experienced no less stress than they did at a lower income level. See Daniel Kahneman and Angus Deaton, "High income improves evaluation of life but not emotional well-being," Proceedings of the National Academy of Sciences, September 7, 2010, doi: 10.1073/pnas.1011492107.

6  James A. Davis, Tom W. Smith, and Peter V. Marsden, *General Social Surveys, 1972–2004* (Roper Center for Public Opinion Research, University of Connecticut, 2004).

7  Richard Easterlin, "The Worldwide Standard of Living Since 1800," *Journal of Economic Perspectives* 14, no. 1 (2000): 7–26

8  Philip Brickman, Dan Coates, and Ronnie Janoff-Bulman, "Lottery Winners and Accident Victims: Is Happiness Relative?" *Journal of Personality and Social Psychology* 36, no. 8 (1978): 917–927, http://education.ucsb.edu /janeconoley/ed197/documents/brickman_lotterywinnersandaccident victims.pdf

9  Adam Smith, *The Theory of Moral Sentiments* (Oxford University Press, 1759, 1976), 149.

10  Richard Easterlin, "Explaining Happiness," Proceedings of the National Academy of Sciences, 100:19, September 16, 2003, 11176–11183.

11  Roper-Starch Organization, Roper Reports 79-1 (Roper Center, University of Connecticut, 1979).

12  Roper-Starch Organization, Roper Reports 95-1 (Roper Center, University of Connecticut, 1995).

13  George Orwell, *1984*, ed. Erich Fromm (Harcourt, 1949), 58.

14  Darrin M. McMahon, *Happiness: A History* (Atlantic Monthly Press, 2006), 403.

15  1996 General Social Survey. This analysis uses a probit estimation to model the likelihood of saying one is "very happy" on a dummy variable indicating one feels "very successful" or "completely successful," income, and the other demographics listed. The coefficients are evaluated at the margin using the mean value of the regressors. James A. Davis, Tom W. Smith, and Peter V. Marsden, *General Social Surveys, 1972–2004* (Storrs, Conn.: The Roper Center for Public Opinion Research, University of Connecticut, 2004).

16  John Mirowsky and Catherine E. Ross. Aging, Status, and Sense of Control (ASOC), 1995, 1998, 2001 [United States] [Computer file]. ICPSR03334-v2. Ohio State University [producer], 2001. Ann Arbor, MI: Inter-university Consortium for Political and Social Research [distributor], 2005-12-15. In these data, people were asked whether they agreed or disagreed with the statement that they were responsible for their own successes. Those who "agreed" or "agreed strongly" said they felt sad, on average, 0.96 days per week. Those who "disagreed" or "disagreed strongly" were sad an average of 1.2 days per week.

17  Joseph A. Schumpeter, *The Theory of Economic Development*, trans. R. Opie (Harvard University Press, 1934).

18  "BET's Robert Johnson to Obama: Stop Attacking the Wealthy," Real Clear Politics Video, October 2, 2011, http://www.realclearpolitics.com/video/2011 /10/02/bets_robert_johnson_to_obama_stop_attacking_the_wealthy.html

19  James A. Davis, Tom W. Smith, and Peter V. Marsden, *General Social Surveys, 1972–2006* (Storrs, Conn.: The Roper Center for Public Opinion Research, University of Connecticut, 2006).

20 J. J. Froh, J. Fan, R. A. Emmons, G. Bono, E. S. Huebner, and P. Watkins, "Measuring Gratitude in Youth: Assessing the Psychometric Properties of Adult Gratitude Scales in Children and Adolescents," *Psychological Assessment*, March 28, 2011, advance online publication, doi: 10.1037/a0021590.

21 In this analysis, I ran a logit model of the binary variable "very happy" on age and a full battery of demographic covariates, using the 2004 GSS data. Using the fitted values of the regression, I calculated the first-order conditions, found the minimum happiness level with respect to age, and showed with the second-order conditions that it is a global minimum. Data: GSS 2004. James A. Davis, Tom W. Smith, and Peter V. Marsden, *General Social Surveys, 1972–2006* (Storrs, Conn.: The Roper Center for Public Opinion Research, University of Connecticut, 2006).

22 Steven F. Maier and Martin E. Seligman, "Learned helplessness: Theory and evidence," *Journal of Experimental Psychology* 105, no. 1 (March 1976): 3–46, doi: 10.1037/0096-3445.105.1.3.

23 M. Seligman and Steven Maier, "Failure to escape traumatic shock," *Journal of Experimental Psychology* 74, no. 1 (May 1967): 1–9.

24 M. Seligman and Donald Hiroto, "Generality of learned helplessness in man," *Journal of Personality and Social Psychology* 31, no. 2 (February 1975): 311–327. See also Thomas O'Rourke, Warren Tryon, and Charles Raps, "Learned helplessness, depression, and positive reinforcement," *Cognitive Therapy and Research* 4, no. 2 (1980): 201–209.

25 John Tierney, "A New Gauge to See What's Beyond Happiness," *New York Times*, May 17, 2011, http://www.nytimes.com/2011/05/17/science/17tierney.html?pagewanted=all

26 Andrew Biggs and Jason Richwine, "Comparing Federal and Private Sector Compensation," American Enterprise Institute, Economic Policy Working Paper 2011-02, http://www.aei.org/docLib/AEI-Working-Paper-on-Federal-Pay-May-2011.pdf

27 Erich Fromm, *Marx's Concept of Man: Milestones of Thoughts in the History of Ideas* (Frederick Ungar Publishing Co., 1961), 29.

28 Work in America, *Report of a Special Task Force to the Secretary of H.E.W.* (MIT Press, 1973).

29 In the words of Alexander Hamilton, "To cherish and stimulate the activity of the human mind, by multiplying the objects of enterprise, is not among the least considerable of the expedients, by which the wealth of a nation may be promoted."Alexander Hamilton, *Report on Manufactures*, December 5, 1791, http://press-pubs.uchicago.edu/founders/documents/v1ch4s31.html

30 Alexis de Tocqueville, *Democracy in America* (1835). Volume 1, book 2.

31 Edward C. Prescott, "Why do Americans work so much more than Europeans?" *Federal Bank of Minneapolis Quarterly Review* 28 (2004): 2–13; Harry Mount, "Take a holiday, companies tell worried American workaholics," *The Telegraph* (UK), August 21, 2006, http://www.telegraph.co.uk/news/1526884/Take-a-holiday-companies-tell-worried-American-workaholics.html

32 Michael Elliott, "Europeans Just Want to Have Fun," *Time*, July 22, 2003, http://www.time.com/time/world/article/0,8599,466081,00.html

33 A. Alesina, R. Di Tella, and R. MacCulloch "Inequality and happiness: Are Europeans and Americans different?" *Journal of Public Economics* 88 (2004): 2009–2042.

34 Prescott, "Why do Americans work so much more than Europeans?"

35 Adam Okulicz-Kozaryn, "Europeans Work to Live and Americans Live to Work (Who Is Happy to Work More: Americans or Europeans?)," *Journal of Happiness Studies* 12 (2011): 225–243.

36 2002 GSS. James A. Davis, Tom W. Smith, and Peter V. Marsden, *General Social Surveys, 1972–2004* (Storrs, Conn.: The Roper Center for Public Opinion Research, University of Connecticut, 2004).

37 Ibid.

38 Ibid.

39 Ibid. Imagine two workers who are identical in every way—same income, education, age, sex, family situation, religion, and politics—but the first is satisfied with his or her job and the second is not. The first person will be 28 percentage points more likely to say he or she is very happy in life. The probit model described regresses a dummy for a response of "very happy" on a dummy for reporting being "very satisfied" or "somewhat satisfied" with one's job, plus all the demographics listed. The coefficients are evaluated at the margin using the mean values of the covariates.

40 Ibid. We can show this statistically by predicting job satisfaction with something unrelated to overall happiness: the answer to the question of whether someone's "main source of satisfaction in life comes from work." If the predicted value of job satisfaction is still related to happiness, it means the former is increasing the latter. Indeed, the statistical analysis shows that this is precisely the case. The procedure to test this hypothesis uses a full-information maximum likelihood tobit model. I regress a 0–2 measure of happiness on a measure of job satisfaction and a vector of demographics; the instrument for job satisfaction is a measure of whether someone says their main source of satisfaction in life comes from work, which is strongly correlated with job satisfaction but largely uncorrelated with general happiness. The resulting coefficient on the predicted value of job satisfaction is large, positive, and significant.

41 1998 GSS. James A. Davis, Tom W. Smith, and Peter V. Marsden, *General Social Surveys, 1972–2004* (Storrs, Conn.: The Roper Center for Public Opinion Research, University of Connecticut, 2004)

42 Adrian White, "University of Leicester produces the first-ever 'world map of happiness,'" University of Leicester press release, International Social Survey Programme, 2002, http://www.eurekalert.org/pub_releases/2006-07/uol-uol072706.php Source: 2002 International Social Survey Program (ISSP). Zentralarchiv für Empirische Sozialforschung.

43 Paramhansa Yogananda, *Autobiography of a Yogi*, preface by W. Y. Evans-Wentz (Rider and Co., 1965).

44 Jonathan V. Last, "Do It Yourself," *Philanthropy Magazine*, Spring 2011, http://www.philanthropyroundtable.org/pdf/1675_63133847.pdf

45 Charles Schwab recounted this to the author.

46 Steven Rogers, *The Entrepreneur's Guide to Finance and Business* (McGraw-Hill: 2002).

47 Cbsalary.com. http://www.cbsalary.com/national-salary-chart.aspx ?specialty=Small+Business+Owner&cty=&sid=&kw=Small+Business +Owner&jn=jn037&edu=&tid=105988

48 W. Mischel, E. B. Ebbesen, and A. R. Zeiss, "Cognitive and attentional mechanisms in delay of gratification," *Journal of Personality and Social Psychology* 21 (1972): 204–218.

49 W. Mischel, Y. Shoda, and Monica Rodriguez, "Delay of gratification in children," *Science* 244, no. 4907 (May 1989): 933–938.

50 Luigi Guiso, Paolo Sapienza, and Luigi Zingales, "Moral and Social Constraints to Strategic Default on Mortgages," National Bureau of Economic Research, Working Paper No. 15145, July 2009, http://www.nber.org /papers/w15145.pdf?new_window=1

51 O. Michel-Kerjan Erwann, "Catastrophe Economics: The National Flood Insurance Program," *Journal of Economic Perspectives* 23, no. 4 (Fall 2010).

52 Matt Cover, "True Cost of Fannie, Freddie Bailouts: $317 billion, CBO says," CNSNews.com, June 6, 2011, http://www.cnsnews.com/news/article /true-cost-fannie-freddie-bailouts-317-bi; Congressional Budget Office Testimony, "The Budgetary Cost of Fannie Mae and Freddie Mac and Options for the Future Federal Role in the Secondary Mortgage Market," June 2, 2011, http://www.cbo.gov/ftpdocs/122xx/doc12213/06-02-GSEs_Testimony.pdf

53 Several estimates find that taxpayers will lose about $14 billion from the automakers' bailout. Devin Dwyer, "How Much Did the Auto Bailout Cost Taxpayers?" abcnews.com Political Punch, June 3, 2011, http://abcnews.go .com/blogs/politics/2011/06/how-much-did-the-auto-bailout-cost-taxpayers/

54 Video available at http://www.nationalreview.com/corner/279808 /ows-protester-wants-college-paid-because-what-he-wants-charles-c-w-cooke

55 "Glenn Beck: Coming nanny state evidence," October 31, 2008. Available at http://www.glennbeck.com/content/articles/article/198/17587/. Video available at http://www.youtube.com/watch?v=Bg98BvqUvCc

56 Kenneth Kaufman, "Tame Duck," Milwaukee Milk Producer, 2, no. 6 (Sept. 1929):4.

CHAPTER THREE

1 See Jonathan Haidt, S. H. Keller, and M. G. Dias, "Affect, Culture, Morality, or Is It Wrong to Eat Your Dog?" *Journal of Personality and Social Psychology* 65, no. 4 (1993): 613–628.

2 Ben Kenward and Matilda Dahl, "Preschoolers distribute scarce resources according to the moral valence of recipients' previous actions," *Developmental Psychology* 47, no. 4 (July 2011): 1054–1064; PsycINFO, EBSCOhost, http://

0-search.ebscohost.com.clark.up.edu/login.aspx?direct=true&db=psyh&AN =2011-10379-001&login.asp?custid=s8474154&site=ehost-live&scope=site

3  Rimma Teper, Michael Inzlicht, and Elizabeth Page-Gould, "Are we more moral than we think?: Exploring the role of affect in moral behavior and moral forecasting," *Psychological Science* 22, no. 4 (2011): 553–558; PsycINFO, EBSCOhost, http://0- search.ebscohost.com.clark.up.edu/login .aspx?direct=true&db=psyh&AN=2011-07884-021&login.asp?custid =s8474154&site=ehost-live&scope=site. The fact that this test was performed in Canada might lead one to ask whether the results would be the same in other countries.

4  See, for example, Laura Seifert, "On H1N1: 'We're Prepared for the Worst,'" http://www.cbsnews.com/stories/2009/09/06/ftn /main5291052.shtml

5  A third definition commonly discussed in the social science literature is reciprocity or the belief that if I do something for you, you should do something for me in exchange.

6  Real Clear Politics Video, October 18, 2010, http://www.realclearpolitics.com /video/2010/10/18/pelosi_need_to_address_fairness_of_ownership_and _equity_in_america.html

7  Barack Obama, "Remarks by the President on International Tax Reform," May 4, 2009, http://www.whitehouse.gov/the_press_office/Remarks-By-The -President-On-International-Tax-Policy-Reform/

8  Milton Friedman and Rose Friedman, *Free to Choose: A Personal Statement* (Harcourt Brace Jovanovich, 1979), 128–149, http://www.vietnamica.net /op/wp-content/uploads/2010/09/Free_To_Choose_Friedman.pdf

9  The higher percentage of rejected offers comes on the East Coast; the lower percentage on the West Coast. Hessel Oosterbeek, Randolph Sloof, and Gijs van de Kuilen, "Cultural Differences in Ultimatum Game Experiments: Evidence from a Meta-Analysis," *Experimental Economics* 7, no. 2, 2004: 171–188, http://0-search.proquest.com.clark.up.edu/docview/222837285 ?accountid=14703

10  To all you experimentalists: I know this does not follow proper experimental protocols, the data are not i.i.d., etc. Keep your shirt on, I'm trying to write an interesting book here.

11  Actually, the big winner is our family dentist.

12  World Values Surveys Databank, "Fairness: One Secretary is Paid More," World Values Survey, United States V115, 2006.

13  Alexis de Tocqueville, *Democracy in America*, (*Literary Classics of the United States*, 2004), 57.

14  Thomas Jefferson, Letter to Joseph Milligan, April 6, 1816. Abraham Lincoln said this in a speech in Connecticut in 1860: "I take it that it is best for all to leave each man free to acquire property as fast as he can. Some will get wealthy. I don't believe in a law to prevent a man from getting rich; it would do more harm than good. So while we do not propose any war upon capital, we do wish to allow the humblest man an equal chance to get rich with everybody else." At this, the crowd broke into thunderous applause.

Abraham Lincoln, "Speech at New Haven, Connecticut," March 6, 1860, *The Collected Works of Abraham Lincoln*, vol.4, ed. Roy P. Basler (Abraham Lincoln Association, 1953), 24.

15 Venture capitalist Kip Hagopian deals eloquently with issues of luck in the case of progressive taxation. See Kip Hagopian, "The Inequity of the Progressive Income Tax," *Policy Review*, no. 166 (April 1, 2011), http://www.hoover.org/publications/policy-review/article/72291

16 Mark Perry, "Income Mobility in the Dynamic U.S. Economy," The Enterprise Blog, March 29, 2011, http://blog.american.com/2011/03/income-mobility-in-the-dynamic-u-s-economy/

17 Daniel P. McMurrer and Isabel C. Sawhill, "Economic Mobility in the United States," Urban Institute, October 1, 1996, http://www.urban.org/publications/406722.html

18 Isabel V. Sawhill and Mark Condon, "Is U.S. Income Inequality Really Growing?: Sorting Out the Fairness Question," *Policy Bites* (Urban Institute, 1992).

19 Richard V. Burkhauser, Douglas Holtz-Eakin, and Stephen E. Rhody, "Labor Earnings Mobility in the United States and Germany During the Growth Years of the 1980s," mimeo, Syracuse University, 1996.

20 Charles Murray, *Losing Ground* (Basic Books, 1984).

21 Jeffrey Stonecash, "Inequality and the American Public," Campbell Public Affairs Institute, Maxwell Poll on Civic Engagement and Inequality, Syracuse University, Maxwell School of Citizenship and Public Affairs, 2005.

22 James Allan Davis, Tom W. Smith, and Peter V. Marsden, "Cumulative Codebook," *General Social Survey (1972–2008)* (National Opinion Research Center, 2008).

23 The World Values Survey asked respondents to answer these questions on a 1–10 scale, where a response of 1 signified "in the long run, hard work usually brings a better life," while 10 meant, "hard work doesn't generally bring success—it's more a matter of luck and connections." Americans were more than twice as likely to give an answer of 1 or 2 than the French were. World Values Surveys Databank, "Hard Work Brings Success," World Values Survey, United States, 2006.

24 Mark Baisley, "Towards More South Park Conservatives," townhall.com, July 17, 2011, http://finance.townhall.com/columnists/markbaisley/2011/07/17/towards_more_south_park_conservatives/page/full/

25 If a liberal and a conservative are exactly identical in income, education, sex, family situation, and race, the liberal will still be 20 percentage points less likely than the conservative to say that hard work leads to success among the disadvantaged. Campbell Public Affairs Institute, Maxwell Poll on Civic Engagement and Inequality [dataset], 2005, Syracuse University, Maxwell School of Citizenship and Public Affairs. These results are based on a probit model in which the beliefs about the importance of hard work are regressed on political views, as well as a vector of demographics. The marginal coefficients are estimated at the mean values of the regressors.

26  Joyce Bryant, "Immigration in the United States," Yale-New Haven Teachers Institute, 2001, http://www.yale.edu/ynhti/curriculum/units/1999/3/99.03.01 .x.html

27  Abraham Lincoln, "Speech at New Haven, Connecticut," March 6, 1860, *The Collected Works of Abraham Lincoln*, vol. 4, ed. Roy P. Basler (Abraham Lincoln Association, 1953), 24. Further, Lincoln believed, "The hired laborer of yesterday, labors on his own account to-day; and will hire others to labor for him tomorrow." See Abraham Lincoln, "Fragment on Free Labor," September 17, 1859, *The Collected Works of Abraham Lincoln*, vol. 3, ed. Roy P. Basler (Abraham Lincoln Association, 1953), 462.

28  "Subjective Class Identification," General Social Survey, Dataset: General Social Survey, 1972–2006, http://www.norc.uchicago.edu/GSS+Website /Browse+GSS+Variables/Mnemonic+Index/

29  The increase inequality referenced here is based on Gini coefficients. The Gini coefficient for the United States grew from 0.401 in 1972 to 0.462 in 2002. "Income, Poverty, and Health Insurance Coverage in the United States: 2009," U.S. Census Bureau, September 2010, http://www.census.gov/prod /2010pubs/p60-238.pdf

30  "Subjective Class Identification," General Social Survey, Dataset: General Social Survey, 1972–2006, http://www.norc.uchicago.edu/GSS+Website /Browse+GSS+Variables/Mnemonic+Index/

31  Karlyn Bowman, "What Do Americans Think About Taxes?" Tax Notes, April 6, 2009, pp. 99–105.

32  Mads Meier Jæger, "'A Thing of Beauty Is a Joy Forever'?: Returns to Physical Attractiveness over the Life Course," *Social Forces* 89, no. 3 (March 2011): 983–1003.

33  Alberto Alesina and George-Marios Angeletos, "Fairness and Redistribution," *American Economic Review* 95, no. 4 (2005): 960–980.

34  James Pethokoukis, "5 reasons why income inequality is a myth–and Occupy Wall Street is wrong," The Enterprise blog, October 18, 2011, http://blog .american.com/2011/10/5-reasons-why-income-inequality-is-a-myth-and -occupy-wall-street-is-wrong/; Robert J. Gordon, "Misperceptions about the Magnitude and Timing of Changes in American Income Inequality," NBER working paper 15351, September 2009, http://www.nber.org/papers/w15351 .pdf?new_window=1. Federal Reserve Bank of Minneapolis economists found that when controlling for key factors, the median household income for almost all household types increased between 44 percent and 62 percent from 1976 to 2006. They observed that the studies that showed much smaller increases in median household income got those results because they didn't control for key factors such as household size or demographic changes over time. Terry J. Fitzgerald, "Where Has All the Income Gone?" *The Region*, September 2008, http://www.minneapolisfed.org/pubs/region/08-09 /income.pdf

35  Richard Burkhauser, "Recent Trends in Top Income Shares in the USA: Reconciling Estimates from March CPS and IRS Tax Return Data," *Review of Economics and Statistics*, forthcoming.

36  Congressional Budget Office, "Trends in the Distribution of Income Between 1979 and 2007," October 2011, http://www.cbo.gov/ftpdocs/124xx /doc12485/10-25-HouseholdIncome.pdf. The data extend only until 2007. We do not have evidence to suggest that the pattern has changed since that time.

37  Arthur M. Okun, *Equality and Efficiency* (Brookings Institution, 1975), 47.

38  Kipling, Rudyard (1919). "The Gods of the Copybook Headings" (poem). http://www.kipling.org.uk/poems_copybook.htm


CHAPTER FOUR

 1  Luke 10: 29–37.

 2  Dan Gilgoff, "New budget campaign asks 'What would Jesus cut?'" CNN.com Belief Blog, February 28, 2011, http://religion.blogs.cnn.com/2011/02/28 /new-budget-campaign-asks-what-would-jesus-cut/

 3  Marco Rubio, address on the proper role of government, Ronald Reagan Presidential Library, August 23, 2011, http://rubio.senate.gov/public /index.cfm/2011/8/icymi-senator-rubio-at-the-reagan-library

 4  Gregory Clark, *A Farewell to Alms: A Brief Economic History of the World* (Princeton University Press, 2007), chapter 1.

 5  M. Dorothy George, *London Life in the Eighteenth Century* (Academy Chicago Publishers, 1985), 42; see also Mabe C. Buer, *Health, Wealth, and Population in the Early Days of the Industrial Revolution, 1760–1815* (George Routledge and Sons, 1926), 30.

 6  George, *London Life in the Eighteenth Century*, 42.

 7  Michael Novak, *Three in One: Essays on Democratic Capitalism 1976–2000*, ed. Edward W. Younkins (Rowman and Littlefield Publishers, 2001), 57.

 8  U.S. Census Bureau, Income data historical tables, "Table P-1. Total CPS Population and Per Capita Income," http:// www.census.gov/hhes/www /income/data/historical/people

 9  Angus Maddison, "Statistics on World Population and Per Capita GDP, 1-2008 AD," http://www.ggdc.net/MADDISON/oriindex.htm. Material progress is tied to technological advances in society, and technological progress has skyrocketed over the last two centuries. The average annual rate of such progress before 1800 was less than 0.05 percent. The rate today is thirty times higher. See Clark, *A Farewell to Alms*.

10  Maddison,"Statistics on World Population and Per Capita GDP, 1-2008 AD."

11  World Bank World Development Indicators, "Life Expectancy at Birth, total (years)," http://data.worldbank.org/indicator/SP.DYN.LE00.IN

12  U.S. Census Bureau. "Series H 664-668. Percent Illiterate in the Population, by Race and Nativity: 1870 to 1969." Bicentennial Edition: Historical Statistics of the United States, Colonial Times to 1970," http://www.census.gov /prod/www/abs/statab.html

13  Steckel, "A History of the Standard of Living in the United States." EH.net Encyclopedia, edited by Robert Whaples, July 21, 2002, http://eh.net/ encyclopedia/article/steckel.standard.living.us

14 "Massachusetts Acts to Save Country's First Public High School," *New York Times*, April 28, 2007, http://www.nytimes.com/2007/04/28/education /28boston.html; Kern Alexander and David M. Alexander, *American Public School Law*, 6th ed. (Thomson West, 2005).

15 In Gregory Clark's words, "[T]he biggest beneficiary of the Industrial Revolution so far has been the unskilled. There have been benefits aplenty for the typically wealthy owners of land or capital, and for the educated. But industrialized economies saved their best gifts for the poorest." Clark, *A Farewell to Alms: A Brief Economic History of the World*, Chapter 1.

16 Maxim Pinkovskiy and Xavier Sala-i-Martin, "Parametric Estimations of the world distribution of income," NBER Working Paper 15433, http://www.nber.org/papers/w15433.pdf

17 Michael Novak, *The Spirit of Democratic Capitalism* (Simon & Schuster, 1982).

18 World Bank, "Country Brief: China," http://web.worldbank.org/WBSITE /EXTERNAL/COUNTRIES/EASTASIAPACIFICEXT/CHINAEXTN /0,,menuPK:318960~pagePK:141132~piPK:141107~theSitePK:318950,00 .html; Arthur C. Brooks, "Don't Live Simply," AEI Articles and Commentary, September 15, 2008, http://www.aei.org/article/28626

19 World Bank, "Dramatic Decline in Global Poverty, but Progress Uneven," April 23, 2004, http://go.worldbank.org/84RMEOWD20

20 World Bank World Development Indicators and Global Development Finance, "GNI Per Capita, Atlas Method (current US$)," http://www .databank.worldbank.org/ddp/home.do

21 Ibid.

22 Hernando de Soto, *The Mystery of Capital: Why Capitalism Triumphs in the West and Fails Everywhere Else* (Basic Books, 2000).

23 Dambisa Moyo, *Dead Aid: Why Aid Is Not Working and How There is a Better Way for Africa* (Farrar, Straus and Giroux, 2009).

24 George Ayittey, a professor of economics at American University and a native of Ghana, has described the continent's challenges: "The problem that happened after independence was that our leaders rejected the market system as a Western institution and tried to destroy it and they also rejected democracy. This is why the continent started its road to ruination." Renee Montagne and George Ayittey, "Expert: Africa Needs More than Foreign Aid," National Public Radio, July 6, 2005, http://npr.org/templates/story/story.php ?storyID=4731168

25 William R. Easterly, "Why Bill Gates Hates My Book," *Wall Street Journal*, February 7, 2008.

26 "Worst of the Worst 2011: The World's Most Repressive Societies," Freedom House Special Report. http://www.freedomhouse.org/uploads/special _report/101.pdf

27 In 2010 GDP terms. See https://www.cia.gov/library/publications /the-world-factbook/geos/ks.html; in GDP per capita terms, it is forty-fifth.

28  North Korea's GDP per capita in 2010 is estimated at $1,800, while South Korea's is $30,000 at Purchasing Power Parity.

29  James Gwartney, Joshua Hall, and Robert Lawson, *Economic Freedom of the World 2010 Annual Report*, Fraser Institute, http://www.fraserinstitute.org /uploadedFiles/fraser-ca/Content/research-news/research/publications /economic-freedom-of-the-world-2010.pdf

30  Economists Hugo Faria and Hugo Montesinos test the causal link between the Economic Freedom of the World (EFW) Index and economic growth. They use instrumental variables to isolate the exogenous sources of variation in the relationship. They report the existence of a strong, positive, statistically significant and economically consequential impact of EFW on growth and average income. Hugo Faria and Hugo Montesinos, "Does economic freedom cause prosperity? An IV approach," *Public Choice* 141, no.1/2 (2009): 103–127.

31  U.S. Census Bureau income data, http://www.census.gov/hhes/www /income/data/historical/inequality/index.html.

32  W. Michael Cox and Richard Alm, "You Are What You Spend," *New York Times*, February 10, 2008.

33  Robert Rector and Rachel Sheffield, "Air Conditioning, Cable TV, and an Xbox: What Is Poverty in the United States Today?" *Backgrounder*, no. 2575, July 18, 2011, http://www.heritage.org/Research/Reports/2011/07 /What-is-Poverty

34  Andy Warhol, *The Philosophy of Andy Warhol (From A to B & Back Again)* (Harcourt Brace Jovanovich, 1975).

35  Whole Foods CEO John Mackey eloquently links economic enrichment and altruism: "Resting everything on self-interest is relying on a very incomplete theory of human nature. . . . People do things for lots of reasons. A false dichotomy is often set up between self-interest, or selfishness, and altruism. To me it is a false dichotomy, because we're obviously both. We are self-interested, but we're not just self-interested. We also care about other people. We usually care a great deal about the well being of our families. We usually care about our communities and the larger society that we live in. We can also care about the well being of animals and our larger environment. We have ideals that motivate us to try to make the world a better place. By a strict definition, they would seem to contradict self-interest, unless you get back into the circular argument that everything you care about and want to do is self-interest." John Mackey, "Defending the Morality of Capitalism," June 24, 2011, http://www2.wholefoodsmarket.com/blogs/jmackey /category/conscious-capitalism/

36  Arthur C. Brooks, *Who Really Cares: The Surprising Truth About Compassionate Conservatism* (Basic Books, 2006).

37  Charitable contributions from American individuals, corporations, and foundations were an estimated $290.89 billion in 2010, up from a revised estimate of $280.30 billion for 2009. The 2010 estimate represents growth of 3.8 percent in current dollars and 2.1 percent in inflation-adjusted dollars. The Center on Philanthropy at Indiana University, June 20, 2011,

http://www .philanthropy.iupui.edu/news/2011/06/pr-GUSA.aspx; International Monetary Fund World Economic Outlook Database, April 2011 Edition, http://www.imf.org/external/pubs/ft/weo/2011/01/weodata/index.aspx

38 Brooks, *Who Really Cares: The Surprising Truth About Compassionate Conservatism.*

39 Ibid.

40 Ibid. All these results come from analysis of the National Opinion Research Center's *General Social Survey* and other publicly available, non-partisan data sources. A large difference persists even after correcting for income differences and other demographics like age and education.

41 1996 and 2002 General Social Survey, National Opinion Research Center, University of Chicago.

42 Lawrence T. White, Raivo Valk, and Abdessamad Dialmy, "What Is the Meaning of 'on Time'? The Sociocultural Nature of Punctuality," *Journal of Cross-Cultural Psychology* 42, no. 3 (April 2011): 482–493.

43 Ralph Nader, speaking at the NAACP's 91st Annual Convention, Baltimore, Maryland, July 11, 2000.

44 Video, http://dailycaller.com/2011/11/17/patriotic-millionaires-demand -higher-taxes-but-unwilling-to-pay-up-video/

45 This conclusion is the product of a two-stage least squares regression, in which income is regressed on a vector of demographics and a fitted value of charitable donations. This fitted value comes from a regression of donations on volunteer time plus appropriate demographics.

46 Tiffany Field, Maria Hernandez-Reif, Olga Quintino, Saul Schanberg, and Cynthia Kuhn, "Elder retired volunteers benefit from giving massage therapy to infants," *Journal of Applied Gerontology* 17 (1998): 229–239.

47 James Morgan, "Too good to be true? Altruism's better for you," *The Herald* (UK), October 26, 2006. The election of the biggest giver as group leader was repeated in other popularity contests, with the more selfish in the group routinely shunned.

48 I infer causality through the use of Granger tests.

49 Christina Romer and Jared Bernstien, "Job Impact of the American Recovery and Reinvestment Plan," January 9, 2009, http://otrans.3cdn.net /45593e8ecbd339d074_l3m6bt1te.pdf; Mark Zandi, "A Second Quick Boost From Government Could Spark Recovery," edited excerpts of testimony before the U.S. House Committee on Small Business, July 24, 2008, http://www.economy.com/mark-zandi/documents/Small%20Business _7_24_08.pdf; Robert J. Barro, "Government Spending Is No Free Lunch," *Wall Street Journal*, January 22, 2009, http://online.wsj.com/article /SB123258618204604599.html; Andrew Mountford and Harald Uhlig, "What Are the Effects of Fiscal Policy Shocks?" SFB 649, Discussion Paper 2005-039, 2005, http://sfb649.wiwi.hu-berlin.de/papers/pdf /SFB649DP2005-039.pdf

50 2000 Social Capital Community Benchmark Survey, Roper Center, University of Connecticut. The same thing happens with gifts of time. Imagine two people

who are identical in terms of income, education, age, religion, politics, sex, and family situation, but one of them volunteers once more a week than the other. That person will be half again as likely to say he or she is "very happy."

51 David Sloan Wilson and Mihaly Csikszentmihalyi, "Health and the Ecology of Altruism," *The Science of Altruism and Health*, ed. S. G. Post (Oxford University Press, 2006), 6.

52 Rodney Balko, "The Road to Hell . . ." Reason.com, November 29, 2006, http://reason.com/blog/2006/11/29/the-road-to-hell. The 2006 law has since been reversed.

53 "Euro area unemployment at 10.0%," Eurostat, August 31, 2011, http://epp.eurostat.ec.europa.eu/cache/ITY_PUBLIC/3-31082011-BP/EN /3-31082011-BP-EN.PDF

CHAPTER FIVE

1 Frank Newport, "Socialism Viewed Positively by 36% of Americans," Gallup.com, February 4, 2010, http://www.gallup.com/poll/125645 /Socialism-Viewed-Positively-Americans.aspx

2 "Entrepreneurship in the EU and Beyond," *Flash Eurobarometer*, December 2009, http://ec.europa.eu/enterprise/policies/sme/facts-figures-analysis /eurobarometer/fl283_en.pdf; "AEI Political Report: The Entrepreneurial Spirit," *American Enterprise Institute for Public Policy Research*, June 2011, http://www.aei.org/docLib/PR-June-2011.pdf

3 *Washington Post*–ABC News Poll, January 12–15, 2010, question 40, http://www.washingtonpost.com/wp-srv/politics/polls/postpoll_011610.html

4 NBC News/*Wall Street Journal* Survey, Study #11091, February 2011, http:// online.wsj.com/public/resources/documents/wsj-nbcpoll03022011.pdf

5 According to Gallup in 2011, 47 percent agreed with this statement, versus 49 percent who disagreed. Lydia Saad, "Americans Divided on Taxing the Rich to Redistribute Wealth," Gallup.com, June 2, 2011, http://www.gallup .com/poll/147881/Americans-Divided-Taxing-Rich-Redistribute-Wealth.aspx

6 Lydia Saad, "Americans Express Historic Negativity Toward U.S. Government," Gallup.com, September 26, 2011, http://www.gallup.com/poll/149678 /Americans-Express-Historic-Negativity-Toward-Government.aspx?utm _source=tagrss&utm_medium=rss&utm_campaign=syndication

7 Woodrow Wilson, "Socialism and Democracy," August 22, 1887. In Arthur S. Link, ed,. *The Papers of Woodrow Wilson*, vol. 5 (Princeton University Press, 1966–1993).

8 Woodrow Wilson, "The Study of Administration," *Political Science Quarterly* 2, no. 2 (June 1887), 197–222. http://www.jstor.org/stable/2139277 ?origin=JSTOR-pdf&. In his essay "The Study of Administration," Wilson laid out definitions of administration science ("a few steady, infallible, placidly wise maxims of government into which all sound political doctrine would be ultimately resolvable") and an administrative cadre ("A corps of civil servants prepared by special schooling and drilled, after appointment, into a perfected organization, with appropriate hierarchy and characteristic

discipline . . . serving with good behavior . . . meaning steady, hearty allegiance to the policy of government . . .").

9  Author's calculations using Office of Management and Budget "The Budget of the United States of America" historical tables. http://www.whitehouse .gov/omb/budget/Historicals

10  Ibid.

11  Leverett S. Lyon, et al., "The National Recovery Administration: An Analysis and Appraisal," Brookings Institution, 1935, 873.

12  Amity Shlaes, *The Forgotten Man: A New History of the Great Depression*, by (HarperCollins, 2007).

13  Ronald Reagan, "State of the Union Address: 1988 Ronald Reagan," *State of the Union Address Library,* January 25, 1988, http://stateoftheunionaddress .org/category/ronald-reagan

14  "NIPA Tables: Table 3.1 Government Current Receipts and Expenditures," *Bureau of Economic Analysis*, data, http://www.bea.gov/iTable/iTable.cfm ?ReqID=9&step=1. Also, for these facts I am grateful to Wisconsin Senator Ron Johnson and his staff.

15  "Economic Outlook No 88–December 2010–OLIS version," *OECD*, Current disbursements, general government, as a percentage of GDP, http://stats .oecd.org/index.aspx?r=33156.

16  Data comes from the Office of Management and Budget Historical Tables (Federal Spending) and the Bureau of Economic Analysis NIPA tables (state and local) for the period 1930–2010. Federal spending and GDP are projected by the CBO in the June 2011 Long-Term Budget Outlook alternative fiscal scenario. State spending is projected by pegging the rate of social benefits growth to federal medical entitlement growth, and pegging the rate of all other state spending growth to other federal noninterest spending growth. Spending prior to 1928 is estimated using the Historical Statistics of the United States Millennial Edition Online by averaging the growth across years using the available data. GDP estimates are from BEA NIPA tables for the period 1929–2010. GDP estimates prior to 1929 use GNP Estimates from Christina Romer, "World War I and the Postwar Depression: A Reinterpretation Based on Alternative Estimates of GNP," *Journal of Monetary Economics* 22 (July 1988): 91–115.
    "NIPA Tables: Table 3.1 Government Current Receipts and Expenditures," Bureau of Economic Analysis, data, http://www.bea.gov/iTable /iTable.cfm ?ReqID=9&step=1;
    "Office of Management and Budget Historical Tables: Table 1.1–Summary of Outlays, Surpluses or Deficits (-): 1789-2016," OMB, February 14, 2011, http://www.whitehouse.gov/omb/budget/Historicals; "CBO's 2011 Long-Term Budget Outlook." Congressional Budget Office. June 22, 2011. http://www.cbo.gov/ftpdocs/122xx/doc12212/06-21-Long-Term_Budget _Outlook.pdf

17  NBC News/*Wall Street Journal* Survey Study #11579, Hart/McInturff, November 22, 2011. Available at http://www.scribd.com/doc/72058015 /NBC-Wall-Street-Journal-11-8-11

18  Tax Foundation. "Federal Individual Income Tax Returns with Zero or Negative Tax Liability," October 18, 2011. http://taxfoundation.org/files /fed_incometax_nonpayer_data_1950-2009-20111018.pdf.

19  Urban-Brookings Tax Policy Center MicroSimulation Model (version 0411-2), "Table T11-0173: Tax Units with Zero or Negative Tax Liabiilty, 2004–2011." http://www.taxpolicycenter.org/numbers/Content/PDF/T11-0173.pdf.

20  "Memorandum: Information on Income Tax Liability for Tax Year 2009," Congress of the United States, Joint Committee on Taxation, April 29, 2011, http://taxprof.typepad.com/files/jct-analysis-2009-income-tax.pdf. Of course, many Americans pay payroll taxes. But this is forced savings, not support for general government services.

21  Matt Moon, "Special Report: How Do Americans Feel About Taxes Today," *Tax Foundation*, April 2009, no. 166, http://www.taxfoundation.org/files /sr166.pdf

22  Scott A.Hodge, "Accounting for What Families Pay for Taxes and What They Receive in Government Spending," *Tax Foundation*, September 21, 2009, Fiscal Fact no. 189, http://www.taxfoundation.org/publications/show/25195 .html

23  Gerand Prante and Mark Robyn, "Summary of Latest Federal Individual Income Tax Data," Tax Foundation Fiscal Facts, October 6, 2010. http:// www.taxfoundation.org/news/show/250.html

24  Congressional Budget Office, "Average Federal Tax Rates in 2007," June 2010. http://www.cbo.gov/ftpdocs/115xx/doc11554/AverageFederalTaxRates2007 .pdf

25  Kip Hagopian has argued convincingly that the progressive income tax is "plainly inequitable." Such inequality becomes clear when the importance of work effort—defined as the number hours worked and the intensity of the effort applied during those hours—is considered. Hagopian argues that, when considering these data, the progressive tax punishes those who work more. In fact, the most equitable system is one based on the value of benefits received from the government. Kip Hagopian, "The Inequity of the Progressive Income Tax," http://www.scribd.com/fullscreen/5192761

26  OECD Tax Database, www.oecd.org/ctp/taxdatabase. Even more important, the U.S. average marginal tax rate is also well above the mean for the countries of the Organization for Economic Cooperation and Development (OECD). Aparna Mathur, "Race to the Top of the Laffer Curve," American.com, February 16, 2011, http://www.american.com/archive/2011 /february/race-to-the-top-of-the-laffer-curve

27  OECD Tax Database, "2010 Top Statutory Rate Table," table 11.1, www.oecd .org/dataoecd/26/56/33717459.xls

28  Nicole V. Crain, and W. Mark Crain, "The Impact of Regulatory Costs on Small Firms," *Small Business Administration, Office of Advocacy,* September 2010, http://archive.sba.gov/advo/research/rs371tot.pdf

29  "National Economic Accounts: Gross Domestic Product," *Bureau of Economic Analysis,* data, http://www.bea.gov/national/index.htm#gdp; "The Budget and Economic Outlook: Fiscal Years 2011 to 2021," *Congressional*

*Budget Office*, January 2011, http://www.cbo.gov/ftpdocs/120xx/doc12039
/01-26_FY2011Outlook.pdf; "Reducing the Deficit: Spending and Revenue
Options," Congressional Budget Office, March 2011, http://www.cbo.gov
/ftpdocs/120xx/doc12085/03-10-ReducingTheDeficit.pdf

30  Scott Shane, "Small Businesses, Big Regulatory Problem," *The American*,
January 20, 2011, http://www.american.com/archive/2011/january
/small-business-big-regulatory-burden

31  Susan Dudley and Melinda Warren, "Fiscal Stalemate Reflected in Regula-
tors' Budget: An Analysis of the U.S. Budget for Fiscal Years 2011 and 2012,"
*The George Washington University* and *Washington University in St.
Louis*, May 2011, http://wc.wustl.edu/files/wc/2012_Regulators_Budget_2_1.pdf

32  As of 2 December 2011. The current debt estimate comes from http://www
.brillig.com/debt_clock/

33  Author's calculation using Congressional Budget Office 2001 Long-Term
Budget Outlook Alternative Fiscal Scenario, http://www.cbo.gov/doc.cfm
?index=12212

34  Ana Lucia Iturriza, International Institute of Social Studies of Erasmus
University Rotterdam, http://www.iss.nl/fileadmin/ASSETS/iss/Documents
/Scholas/An_Exercise_in_Worldmaking_2005-2006.pdf

35  A. Bergh and M. Henrekson, "Government Size and Growth: A Survey and
Interpretation of Evidence," *Journal of Economic Surveys*. (June 2011),
doi: 10.1111/j.1467-6419.2011.00697.x.

36  For a sample of the literature, see Y. Algan, , P. Cahuc, and A. Zylberberg,
"Public Employment and Labor Market Preferences." *Economic Policy*,
(2002): 1–65. T. Conley, and B. Dupor, "The American Recovery and
Reinvestment Act: Public Sector Jobs Saved, Private Sector Jobs Forestalled."
May 2011. http://web.econ.ohio-state.edu/dupor/arra10_may11.pdf;
J.Malley, and T. Moutos, "Government Employment and Unemployment:
With One Hand Giveth, The Other Taketh," University of Glasgow, Working
Paper Series no. 9709, May 1998.

37  "National Economic Accounts: Gross Domestic Product," *Bureau of Economic Analysis*, data, http://www.bea.gov/national/index.htm#gdp.

38  The trendline is calculated using a simple OLS regression.


CHAPTER SIX

1  Thomas Jefferson, First Inaugural Address, March 4, 1801, The Avalon Project at Yale School, http://avalon.law.yale.edu/19th_century/jefinau1.asp.

2  "Now, there are some who question the scale of our ambitions. . . . What the
cynics fail to understand is that the ground has shifted beneath them, that
the stale political arguments that have consumed us for so long no longer
apply. The question we ask today is not whether our government is too big
or too small, but whether it works—whether it helps families find jobs at a
decent wage, care they can afford, a retirement that is dignified." Barack
Obama, Inaugural address, January 21, 2009, http://www.whitehouse.gov
/blog/inaugural-address/

3 See http://www.washingtonpost.com/politics/president-obamas-economic
-speech-in-osawatomie-kans/2011/12/06/gIQAVhe6ZO_print.html

4 Fox News Opinion Dynamics Poll, February 19, 2009, http://www.foxnews
.com/projects/pdf/021909_FNCPoll.pdf

5 "2011 Annual Report of the Boards of Trustees of the Federal Hospital Insurance and Federal Supplementary Medical Insurance Trust Funds," May 13,
2011, https://www.cms.gov/ReportsTrustFunds/downloads/tr2011.pdf

6 Figure reflects total expenditures on Medicaid, Food and Nutrition Assistance, Supplemental Security Income, and Family and Other Support
Assistance. Office of Management and Budget Historical Tables, "Table 8.5–
Outlays for mandatory and related programs: 1962–2016," http://www
.whitehouse.gov/omb/budget/Historicals

7 Adam Smith, *An Inquiry into the Nature and Causes of the Wealth of
Nations*, ed. Sálvio M. Soares (MetaLibri, 2007), v.1.0s.

8 Data for November 2011, "2011 Monthly Medallion 'Non-Accessible' Sales–
Average Prices & Number of Transfers," New York City Taxi & Limousine
Commission, http://www.nyc.gov/html/tlc/downloads/pdf/avg_med_price
_2k11_november.pdf

9 Melissa Kearney, "State Lotteries and Consumer Behavior," NBER Working
Paper 9330, November 2002

10 Ibid.

11 Ronald H. Coase, "The Problem of Social Cost," *Journal of Law and Economics* 3, no. 1 (1960): 1–44.

12 Raquel Girvin, "Aircraft noise-abatement and mitigation strategies," *Journal
of Air Transport Management* 15 (2009): 14–22.

13 Scott Cohn, "CNBC's Top States for Business 2010–And the Winner Is
Texas," cnbc.com, July 13, 2010, http://www.cnbc.com/id/37642856
/CNBC_s_Top_States_For_Business_2010_And_The_Winner_Is_Texas

14 Bureau of Labor Statistics employment data, http://data.bls.gov/cgi-bin
/surveymost?sm+48

15 Mavis Amundson, "Local professor notes Hunthausen's influence," *West
Seattle Herald*, January 11, 1984.

16 Office of Management and Budget, Historical Tables, *Budget of the United
States Government, Fiscal Year 2012*, "Table 3.1–Outlays by Superfunction
and Function: 1940-2016," http://www.whitehouse.gov/omb/budget
/Historicals

17 Economists also note that public goods are "nonrivalrous," meaning that one
person's use does not crowd out another's. For example, the keyboard I am
using right now is rivalrous in that my using it means you can't. In contrast,
my protection by the army right now does not lessen yours.

18 George A. Akerlof, "The Market for 'Lemons': Quality Uncertainty and
the Market Mechanism," *Quarterly Journal of Economics* 84, no. 3 (1970):
488–500.

19  See http://www.washingtonpost.com/politics/president-obamas-economic
    -speech-in-osawatomie-kans/2011/12/06/gIQAVhe6ZO_print.html.

20  Michael Barone, "Federal Expansion the Real Issue in Debt Ceiling Debate,"
    *Washington Examiner,* July 17, 2011.

21  The government is involved, however, if you get a tax deduction for your
    contribution.

22  Alex Pollock, "Lots of Regulatory Expansion but Little Reform," *AEI Regula-
    tion Outlook,* June 2010, http://www.aei.org/docLib/04-RegO-2010-g.pdf

23  Economists have proved that social capital makes people more prosperous,
    too. See Anil Rupasingha, Stephan J. Goetz, and David Freshwater, "Social
    Capital and Economic Growth: A County-Level Analysis," *Journal of Agri-
    cultural and Applied Economics* 32, no. 3 (2000): 565–572.

24  In general, monopoly is the area least mitigated by social capital. But even
    there, trust and social cohesion make people less likely to want to behave in
    a predatory way with competitors and consumers.

25  See http://www.hks.harvard.edu/saguaro/communitysurvey/results_matrix
    .html

26  This wasn't always so. As Charles Murray points out in his 2012 book
    *Coming Apart,* dense urban areas in the past frequently had very high levels
    of social capital. Charles Murray, *Coming Apart: The State of White America,
    1960–2010.* New York: Crown Forum, (2012).

27  Alexis de Tocqueville, *Democracy in America,* ed. J. P. Maier, trans. George
    Lawrence (Anchor Books, 1969).

28  Murray also uses this example in his book *Coming Apart.*

29  Edward C. Banfield, *The Moral Basis of a Backward Society* (Free Press,
    1958).

30  See Arthur C. Brooks, "Is There a Dark Side to Government Support for
    Nonprofits?" *Public Administration Review* 60, no. 3 (2000): 211–218;
    B. Duncan, "Modeling charitable contributions of time and money," *Journal
    of Public Economics* 72, no. 2 (1999): 213–242.

31  James Andreoni and A. Abigail Payne, "Is crowding out due entirely to
    fundraising? Evidence from a panel of charities," *Journal of Public
    Economics* 95 (2011): 334–343.

32  See, in particular, Peter L. Berger and Richard John Neuhaus, *To Empower
    People: from State to Civil Society,* 20th anniversary ed. (American Enter-
    prise Institute Press, 1996).

33  Pope Pius XI, "Quadragesimo Anno," Papal Encyclical, http://www
    .vatican.va/holy_father/pius_xi/encyclicals/documents/hf_p-xi_enc_19310515
    _quadragesimo-anno_en.html.

CHAPTER SEVEN

 1  CNN Opinion Research Corporation poll, June 3–7, 2011,
    http://i2.cdn.turner.com/cnn/2011/images/06/08/june.8.pdf

2 There is overlap in these solutions across issues, because the same policy (for example, repealing Dodd-Frank, or reforming our tax code) can have positive effects on more than one issue. I leave aside energy, health care, and terrorism only because they require much more specialized information and background than I can practically bring to bear in this chapter.

3 Friedman, Benjamin M. (Fall 2005). "The Moral Case for Growth" *The International Economy*, pp. 40–45. http://www.economics.harvard.edu/faculty /friedman/files/The%20Moral%20Case%20for%20Growth.pdf

4 Bureau of Economic Analysis National Economic Accounts, http://www .bea.gov/national/.

5 Author's calculation using Congressional Budget Office 2001 Long-Term Budget Outlook Alternative Fiscal Scenario, http://www.cbo.gov/doc.cfm ?index=12212

6 A common rule of thumb in finance, 72 divided by a growth rate gives the approximate number of periods before an investment doubles. In this case, 72 divided by 1 is 72.

7 The 2005 President's Advisory Panel on Federal Tax Reform shows that a complete shift to consumption taxation "could increase national income by up to 2.3 percent over the [10 year] budget window, by up to 4.5 percent over 20 years, and by up to six percent over the long run." See the President's Advisory Panel on Federal Tax Reform, "Simple, Fair, and Pro-Growth: Proposals to Fix America's Tax System," November 2005, 149, 190, http://www.taxpolicycenter.org/taxtopics/upload/tax-panel-2.pdf

8 Peter J. Wallison, "Dodd-Frank's Threat to Financial Stability," *Wall Street Journal*, March 25, 2011, http://online.wsj.com/article/SB1000142405274870 385840457621419395752740 6.html

9 William Easterly and Sergio Reblo, "Fiscal Policy and Economic Growth: An Empirical Investigation," NBER Working Paper #4499, October 1993; A. Bergh and M. Henrekson, "Government Size and Growth: A Survey and Interpretation of Evidence," *Journal of Economic Surveys*, June 2011, doi: 10.1111/j.1467-6419.2011.00697.x. The two economists reviewed the considerable research on government spending and economic growth, and found that there was a near-consensus in the literature that higher government spending correlates with slower growth.

10 Gary Becker, Steven J.Davis, and Kevin Murphy, "Uncertainty and the Slow Recovery," *Wall Street Journal*, January 4, 2010. http://online.wsj.com /article/SB10001424052748703278604574624711732528426.html

11 Scott R. Baker, Nicholas Bloom, and Steven Davis, "Measuring Economic Policy Uncertainty," September 12, 2011, http://www.stanford.edu/~nbloom /PolicyUncertainty.pdf. The researchers use an empirical model that looks at Google-media data, the number of expiring tax measures, and the level of disagreement among forecasters over future federal government spending and future CPI levels to measure policy uncertainty and calculate its impact on jobs and growth.

12  See Madeline Zavodny, "Immigration and American Jobs," 2011. http://www.aei.org/paper/society-and-culture/immigration/immigration -and-american-jobs/

13  Bureau of Labor Statistics Employment Situation Summary, http://www .bls.gov/news.release/empsit.nr0.htm

14  Ibid.

15  Ibid.

16  Ibid.

17  Ibid.

18  "More Signs That a Generation of Young Americans (18-29) Have Been Left Adrift by Joblessness as Anemic Jobs Numbers Are Released." Generation Opportunity, August 5, 2011. http://generationopportunity.org/press /more-signs-that-a-generation-of-young-americans-18-29-have-been-left -adrift-by-joblessness-as-anemic-jobs-numbers-are-released-generation -opportunity-statement/

19  See Christina Romer and Jared Bernstein, "The Job Impact of the American Recovery and Reinvestment Plan," January 9, 2009, http://www.politico .com/pdf/PPM116_obamadoc.pdf

20  Peter Wallison, "Repeal the Democrat's Complex and Expensive Legislation," theatlantic.com, July 19, 2011, http://www.theatlantic.com/business/archive /2011/07/repeal-the-democrats-complex-and-expensive-legislation/242143/

21  See the following Congressional testimony by economist Douglas Holtz-Eakin: http://waysandmeans.house.gov/UploadedFiles/HoltzEakin _Testimony_1_5.pdf

22  Timothy Conley and Bill Dupor, "The American Recovery and Reinvestment Act: Public Sector Jobs Saved, Private Sector Jobs Forestalled," May 17, 2011, http://web.econ.ohio-state.edu/dupor/arra10_may11.pdf

23  For a sample of the literature, see Y. Algan, P. Cahuc, and A. Zylberberg, "Public Employment and Labor Market Preferences," *Economic Policy* (2002): 1–65; T. Conley and B. Dupor, "The American Recovery and Reinvestment Act: Public Sector Jobs Saved, Private Sector Jobs Forestalled," May 2001, http://web.econ.ohio-state.edu/dupor/arra10_may11.pdf; J. Malley and T. Moutos, "Government Employment and Unemployment: With One Hand Giveth, The Other Taketh," University of Glasgow Working Paper Series no. 9709, May 1998.

24  Department of Energy. September 4, 2009. Available at http://energy.gov/ articles/vice-president-biden-announces-finalized-535-million-loan -guarantee-solyndra.

25  Barack Obama, "Use of Project Labor Agreements for Federal Construction Projects," Executive Order, February 6, 2009; David G. Tuerck, Sarah Glassman, and Paul Bachman, "Project Labor Agreements on Federal Construction Projects: A Costly Solution in Search of a Problem," *The Beacon Hill Institute Policy Study*, August 2009.

26  Joe Nocera, "How Democrats Hurt Jobs," *New York Times*, August 22, 2011, http://www.nytimes.com/2011/08/23/opinion/nocera-how-democrats-hurt-job-creation.html

27  Christopher Hinton, "NLRB drops case against Boeing over S.C. facility," MarketWatch, December 9, 2011, http://www.marketwatch.com/story/nlrb-drops-case-against-boeing-over-sc-facility-2011-12-09

28  Congressional Budget Office, *The Budget and Economic Outlook: An Update*, August 2011, 5, http://www.cbo.gov/ftpdocs/123xx/doc12316/Update_SummaryforWeb.pdf). See also *The Budget and Economic Outlook: Fiscal Years 2011 through 2021*, January 2011, 134, http://www.cbo.gov/ftpdocs/120xx/doc12039/01-26_FY2011Outlook.pdf

29  Carmen M. Reinhart and Kenneth S. Rogoff, "Growth in a Time of Debt," NBER Working Paper, January 2010, http://www.nber.org/papers/w15639

30  Congressional Budget Office, The Budget and Economic Outlook: An Update.

31  Author's calculation. The U.S. deficit for fiscal year 2011 is $1.3 trillion dollars and the current population of the United States is 312,815,221 according to the U.S. Census Bureau.

32  Dana Blanton, "Fox News poll: 79% Say U.S. Economy Could Collapse," FoxNews.com, March 23, 2010, http://www.foxnews.com/politics/2010/03/23/fox-news-poll-say-economy-collapse/#ixzz1hHcXd2Cq

33  Congressional Budget Office, The Budget and Economic Outlook: An Update. This is based on fiscal year 2011.

34  Author's calculation using Congressional Budget Office, Long-Term Budget Outlook, June 2011, Alternative Fiscal Scenario, http://www.cbo.gov/doc.cfm?index=12212

35  Ibid.

36  Andrew G. Biggs, Kevin A. Hassett, and Matthew Jensen, "A Guide for Deficit Reduction in the United States Based on Historical Consolidations That Worked," AEI Economic Policy Working Paper, December 27, 2010, http://www.aei.org/paper/100179

37  Ibid.

38  Daniel Leigh, Pete Devries, Charles Freedman, Jaime Guajardo, and Andrea Pescatori, "Will It Hurt? Macroeconomic Effects of Fiscal Consolidation," *World Economic Outlook: Recovery, Risk, and Rebalancing* (International Monetary Fund, 2010).

39  "The Moment of Truth: Report of the National Commission on Fiscal Responsibility and Reform," December 2010, http://www.fiscalcommission.gov/sites/fiscalcommission.gov/files/documents/TheMomentofTruth12_1_2010.pdf.

40  J. Monke and R. Johnson, *Actual Farm Bill Spending and Cost Estimates* (Congressional Research Service, December 13, 2010).

41  Energy Information Administration, "Federal Financial Interventions and Subsidies in Energy Markets 2007," April 2008, ftp://ftp.eia.doe.gov/service/srcneaf%282008%2901.pdf

42 "The Moment of Truth: Report of the National Commission on Fiscal Responsibility and Reform," December 2010; Paul Ryan, "The Path to Prosperity," April 2011; Fiscal Year 2012 Budget Resolution, http://budget.house .gov/UploadedFiles/PathToProsperityFY2012.pdf

43 "The Moment of Truth: Report of the National Commission on Fiscal Responsibility and Reform," December 2010; Paul Ryan, "The Path to Prosperity," April 2011.

44 C. Eugene Steuerle and Stephanie Rennane, "Social Security and Medicare Taxes and Benefits Over a Lifetime," Urban Institute, June 2011, http:// www.urban.org/UploadedPDF/social-security-medicare-benefits-over -lifetime.pdf

45 Social Security and Medicare Boards of Trustees, "A summary of the 2011 Annual Reports," http://www.socialsecurity.gov/oact/trsum/index.html.

46 Ibid.

47 Author's calculation using Congressional Budget Office, 2001 Long-Term Budget Outlook Alternative Fiscal Scenario, http://www.cbo.gov/doc.cfm ?index=12212

48 U.S. Social Security Administration Office of Retirement and Disability Policy, "Annual Statistical Supplement, 2010," "Table 3.E2–Number and percentage of poor persons, by age, at end of selected years 1959–2008," http://www.ssa .gov/policy/docs/statcomps/supplement/2010/3e.html#table3.e2

49 Update 2011, Social Security Administration, October 2010, http://ssa.gov/pubs/10003.pdf

50 *The 2011 Annual Report of the Board of Trustees of the Federal Old-Age and Survivors Insurance and Federal Disability Insurance Trust Funds*, Table V.A4, "Cohort Life Expectancy," http://www.ssa.gov/OACT/TR/2011/lr5a4.html

51 Ibid.

52 Solvency provision, Social Security Administration, http://www.ssa.gov /OACT/solvency/provisions/charts/chart_run466.html

53 Author's calculations based on Social Security Administration's solvency provision proposals: http://www.ssa.gov/OACT/solvency/provisions/charts/chart_run375.html; http://www.ssa.gov/OACT/solvency/provisions/charts/chart_run211.html; http://www.ssa.gov/OACT/solvency/provisions/charts/chart_run383.html

54 See Joseph Antos, Andrew Biggs, Alex Brill, and Alan D. Viard, "Fiscal Solutions: A Balanced Plan for Fiscal Stability and Economic Growth," Peter G. Peterson Foundation Solutions Initiative, May 25, 2011, http://pgpf.org /Issues/Fiscal-Outlook/2011/01/20/~/media/6A83826740A94DBE91CCA 557ECA1D36F

55 U.S. Social Security Administration Office of Retirement and Disability Policy "Annual Statistical Supplement, 2010," "Table 3.E2–Number and percentage of poor persons, by age, at end of selected years 1959–2008," http:// www.ssa.gov/policy/docs/statcomps/supplement/2010/3e.html#table3.e2

56 Author's calculations based on Paul Van de Water and Arloc Sherman, "Social Security Keeps 20 Million Americnas Out of Poverty: A State-by-

State Analysis," Center on Budget and Policy Priorities, August 11, 2010, http://www.cbpp.org/files/8-11-10socsec.pdf

57  "2011 Annual Report of the Boards of Trustees of the Federal Hospital Insurance and Federal Supplementary Medical Insurance Trust Funds," http://www.cms.gov/ReportsTrustFunds/downloads/tr2011.pdf

58  Kaiser Family Foundation Statehealthfacts.org, "United States: Federal and State Share of Medicaid Spending, FY2009," http://statehealthfacts.org/comparemaptable.jsp?ind=177&cat=4&sub=47&yr=90&typ=4&sort=a&rgnhl=4

59  "Medicaid Enrollment as a Percent of Total Population," The Public Policy Institute of New York State, Inc., http://www.ppinys.org/reports/2010/innovation/MedicaidEnrollment.html; "Federal and State Share of Medicaid Spending," The Henry J. Kaiser Family Foundation, http://statehealthfacts.org/comparetable.jsp?ind=636&cat=4&sub=47&yr=90&typ=4; United States Department of Agriculture Economic Research Service, "State Fact Sheets: New York," updated September 14, 2011, http://www.ers.usda.gov/Statefacts/NY.HTM

60  "2011 Annual Report of the Boards of Trustees of the Federal Hospital Insurance and Federal Supplementary Medical Insurance Trust Funds," http://www.cms.gov/ReportsTrustFunds/downloads/tr2011.pdf

61  Congressional Budget Office, "CBO's 2011 Long Term Budget Outlook," June 2011, http://www.cbo.gov/doc.cfm?index=12212

62  Thomas P. Miller and James Capretta, "Beyond Repeal and Replace: The Defined Contribution Route to Health Care Choice and Competition," AEI Press, 2010, http://www.aei.org/docLib/Defined-Contribution-Route-to-Health-Care-Choice.pdf

63  Matt Moon, "How Do Americans Feel About Taxes Today?" Tax Foundation Special Report No. 166, April 2009, http://www.taxfoundation.org/files/sr166.pdf.

64  Urban-Brookings Tax Policy Center, Table 11-0173, "Tax Units with Zero or Negative Tax Liability, 2004–2011," http://www.taxpolicycenter.org/numbers/Content/PDF/T11-0173.pdf

65  Scott A. Hodge, "Accounting for What Families Pay in Taxes and What They Receive in Government Spending," Tax Foundation Fiscal Fact No. 189, September 21, 2009, http://www.taxfoundation.org/publications/show/25195.html

66  National Taxpayer Advocate Annual Report to Congress, December 31, 2010, http://www.taxpayeradvocate.irs.gov/files/ExecSummary_2010ARC.pdf

67  Ibid.

68  OECD Tax Database, www.oecd.org/ctp/taxdatabase. Even more important, the U.S. average marginal tax rate is also well above the mean for the countries in the Organisation for Economic Co-operation and Development (OECD). Aparna Mathur, "Race to the Top of the Laffer Curve," American.com, February 16, 2011, http://www.american.com/archive/2011/february/race-to-the-top-of-the-laffer-curve

69  Arthur Laffer, "The Laffer Curve: Past, Present, and Future," Heritage Foundation Backgrounder #1765, June 1, 2004, http://www.heritage.org /Research/Reports/2004/06/The-Laffer-Curve-Past-Present-and-Future

70  Kevin Hassett, "Laffer Curve Pays Billions If Obama Just Asks," Bloomberg .com, February 13, 2011, http://www.businessweek.com/news/2011-02-13 /laffer-curve-pays-billions-if-obama-just-asks-kevin-hassett.html; Alex Brill and Kevin A. Hassett, "Revenue-Maximizing Corporate Income Taxes: The Laffer Curve in OECD Countries," AEI Working Paper #137, July 31, 2007.

71  Matthew H. Jensen and Aparna Mathur, "Corporate Tax Burden on Labor: Theory and Empirical Evidence," *Tax Notes*, June 6, 2011, http://www.aei.org /docLib/Tax-Notes-Mathur-Jensen-June-2011.pdf

72  Most economists believe that we are not on the wrong side of the Laffer curve for personal income taxes. However, we are taxing citizens at a level that compromises savings and thus economic growth.

73  Dylan Matthews, "Where does the Laffer curve bend?" Washingtonpost.com, August 9, 2010, http://voices.washingtonpost.com/ezra-klein/2010/08/ where_does_the_laffer_curve_be.html

74  This refers to Title 26 of the US Code of Federal Regulations and Title 26 of the United States Code. See http://bookstore.gpo.gov/baskets/cfr-listing.jsp.

75  Small Business Taxes & Management Special Report, "Expiring Tax Provisions 2009–2020," http://www.smbiz.com/sbspec324.html

76  Joint Committee on Taxation, "Estimates of Federal Tax Expenditures for Fiscal Years 2010–2014," JCS-3-10, December 15, 2010, http://www.jct.gov /publications.html?func=startdown&id=3718.

77  Ibid.

78  See President's Advisory Panel on Federal Tax Reform, *Simple, Fair, and Pro-Growth: Proposals to Fix America's Tax System* (Government Printing Office, 2005), 183. The Progressive Consumption Tax plan did not receive the consensus support from panel members required for it to be officially recommended by the panel. Bracket endpoints are in 2006 dollars; 2012 values would be roughly 15 percent higher. One of the most compelling consumption tax options today is what economists call the Bradford "X tax," named for Princeton economist David Bradford, which is a flat tax on businesss income, plus a mildly progressive tax on private wages. For a more detailed description of the X Tax, see Robert Carroll, Scott Ganz, and Alan D. Viard, "The X Tax: The Progressive Consumption Tax America Needs?" AEI Tax Policy Outlook, December 2008; and Joseph Antos, Andrew Biggs, Alex Brill and Alan D. Viard, "Fiscal Solutions: A Balanced Plan for Fiscal Stability and Economic Growth," Peterson Foundation Solutions Initiative, May 25, 2011.

# INDEX